Anatomy
Mortgage

Understanding and Negotiating
Commercial Real Estate Loans

R. Wilson Freyermuth
John P. McNearney
Debra Pogrund Stark
Dale A. Whitman

Section of Real Property,
Probate and Trust Law

Defending Liberty
Pursuing Justice

Cover design by ABA Publishing

Library of Congress Cataloging-in-Publication Data

Anatomy of a mortgage: understanding and negotiating commercial real estate loans / R. Wilson Freyermuth ... [et al.].
    p. cm.
    Includes index.
    ISBN 1-57073-896-3
    1. Mortgages—United States. 2. Commercial loans—Law and legislation—United States 3. Real estate development—Finance—Law and legislation—United States. I. Freyermuth, R. Wilson, 1962– II. American Bar Association.
KF695 .A85 2001
346.7304'364 — dc21

                                                    2001022131

Table of Contents

Acknowledgments

The genesis for this book was the desire to provide basic, useful information to new lawyers relating to the law of real estate finance. To achieve this goal, the Workouts, Foreclosures, and Bankruptcies Committee of the Real Property, Probate and Trust Law Section of the American Bar Association created a series of programs that would "dissect" a standard form mortgage. The featured speakers of the program provided a basic explanation of the terms of the mortgage and its enforcement. A panel of experts in the areas of bankruptcy law, construction law, securitization, environmental law, and multifamily aspects provided additional commentary on the sections of the form that relate to these specialty areas. Another panelist reviewed the form mortgage from the perspective of a borrower's counsel, identifying those sections that would be problematic and explaining why. The authors of this book would like to thank Pam Belleman, the Chairperson of the Workouts, Foreclosures, and Bankruptcies Committee and the Program Chair, as well as the individuals who served as panelists on the programs that form the basis for this book:

Melanie Rovner Cohen
Alexandra R. Cole
Neil S. Kessler
Jeffrey Lenobel

James C. Ryan, Jr.

Mark S. Shiembob

Stanley P. Sklar

The authors would especially like to thank James C. Ryan, Jr., of the Richmond, Virginia, firm of Mays & Valentine and former Assistant and Deputy Attorney General of the Commonwealth of Virginia, for preparing the commentary on the environmental provisions of the Deed of Trust.

About the Authors

R. Wilson Freyermuth is Associate Professor of Law at the University of Missouri in Columbia. He received a BS in Business Administration from the University of North Carolina at Chapel Hill in 1984, and a JD with highest honors from Duke University School of Law in 1987. After clerking with the Honorable John D. Butzner, Jr., of the United States Court of Appeals for the Fourth Circuit in Richmond, Virginia, Freyermuth worked from 1988 to 1991 with Womble Carlyle Sandridge & Rice in Raleigh, North Carolina, focusing on the areas of commercial real estate, bankruptcy, and federal appellate practice. During 1991–1992, Freyermuth was a visiting lecturer at the University of Denver College of Law. He arrived at the University of Missouri in 1992, where he teaches Property, Secured Transactions, Real Estate Finance, Real Estate Leasing, Real Estate Transactions, and Local Government. He has also been a visiting professor at Duke University School of Law. He serves as a book editor for the Books/Media Products Committee of the ABA Real Property, Probate, and Trust Law Section.

John P. McNearney is a partner in the firm of Blackwell Sanders Peper Martin in St. Louis, Missouri, and is Chairman of the firm's Real Estate Department. He received his BA from the University of Virginia in 1979 and his JD from Northwestern University in 1983. He previously served from 1985 to 1987 as Assistant Counsel of General American

Life Insurance Company and from 1987 to 1992 as Counsel and First Vice President of First Nationwide Bank. Mr. McNearney's representative clients include California Federal Savings Bank, Equitable Life Assurance Society of the United States, General American Life Insurance Company, LaSalle Bank National Association, and Wells Fargo Bank. Mr. McNearney has been a contributing author of several books, including *Real Estate Financing* (Missouri Bar, 2000), *Foreclosure Law and Related Remedies* (ABA, 1995), and *Banking and Lending Institution Forms* (Warren Gorham Lamont, 1992).

Debra Pogrund Stark is Associate Professor of Law at The John Marshall Law School, teaching in the areas of property law and real estate transactions. She has also served as a visiting lecturer at University of Haifa Law School in the spring of 1997 and as Visiting Associate Professor at the Northwestern University School of Law in the spring of 2000. Upon joining the faculty of The John Marshall Law School in 1994, Professor Stark helped to create the school's LL.M. Program in Real Estate. Professor Stark teaches in the program and served on the program's Board of Advisors. Prior to joining the faculty, she practiced with the Chicago firms of Greenberger & Kaufmann and Katten Muchin & Zavis, concentrating in the fields of commercial real estate finance and development. She received her BA in History from Brandeis University, graduating summa cum laude and Phi Beta Kappa. She received her JD cum laude from Northwestern University School of Law, where she was an articles editor on the *Journal of International Law & Business*. Professor Stark has written numerous articles on various facets of commercial real transactions and other topics. Her articles have been published in the *Banking Law Journal; Barrister Magazine; Business Law Today;* the *Journal of Real Estate Development;* the *Journal of International Law & Business; Oklahoma Law Review; Practical Lawyer; Probate & Property; Real Estate Finance;* the *Real Property, Probate & Trust Law Journal; South Carolina Law Review; St. John's Law Review;* and the *University of Michigan Journal of Law Reform*. She is a co-author and editor of several books. Her most recent book, *Commercial Real Estate Transactions: A Project and Skills Oriented Approach*, will be published by Lexis Law Publishing in 2001. She was a contributing editor of the book *Foreclosure Law & Related Remedies: A State-by-State Digest*, published by the American Bar Association in 1995, and the editor and a contributing author of the book *Consensual Transfers of Distressed Real Estate*, published by the American Bar Association in 1998. An active member of ABA, she served as Chairman of the Foreclosure and Related

Remedies Committee of the ABA's Real Property, Probate and Trust Law Section from 1993 to 1997 and as Assistant Secretary of the section in 1998. She is currently a senior editor of the section's Books/Media Program. Professor Stark has participated as program chair, moderator, and panelist on numerous ABA and Real Property Section programs, as well as on programs organized by the American Association of Law Schools and various individual law schools.

Dale A. Whitman is James Campbell Professor of Law at the University of Missouri in Columbia. He received his BES degree in Electrical Engineering from Brigham Young University in 1963 and his law degree from Duke University in 1966. After practicing for a short period with the firm of O'Melveny and Myers in Los Angeles, Whitman began his academic career at the University of North Carolina in 1967. He was a member of the original faculty when the Brigham Young University law school was founded in 1973. He has since been a faculty member at the University of Washington (where he served as associate dean) and the University of Missouri–Columbia (where he served as dean from 1982 to 1988). He has also been a visiting professor at the University of Tulsa, the University of Utah, and UCLA. Whitman's principal fields of interest are property and real estate finance. He is a co-author of five books in these areas and has also written numerous articles. During 1971–1973 he was involved with the nation's federal housing programs, serving in Washington with the Federal Home Loan Bank Board and the Department of Housing and Urban Development. He was co-reporter, with Professor Grant Nelson of UCLA, of the American Law Institute's Restatement (Third) of Property: Mortgages, published in 1997. He was a member of the Executive Committee of the Association of American Law Schools from 1994 through 1997, and will serve as its president for the year 2002. He is currently a member of the Joint Editorial Board for Uniform Real Property Acts and is the reporter for the Uniform Power of Sale Foreclosure Act, currently in the drafting stage. He is a member of the Order of the Coif, the American Law Institute, and the American College of Real Estate Lawyers, and is a Fellow of the American Bar Foundation.

Introduction

This book endeavors to provide an understanding of the basic concepts of real estate finance that a lawyer must know to be an effective counsel to borrowers or lenders in the context of a commercial real estate loan. This book accomplishes this goal through a detailed analysis of a form real estate mortgage. Lawyers new to the practice of real estate finance can benefit greatly from a highly practical evaluation of a commercial form mortgage document that comprehensively addresses all of the important aspects of a mortgage transaction.

The book uses the Federal National Mortgage Association ("Fannie Mae") Deed of Trust form for multifamily housing. The authors selected this form for several reasons. First, the form contemplates income-producing property as collateral, as distinguished from a loan secured by a residence that the borrower will live in. The form thus contains special provisions that relate to the "commercial" nature of the property, such as the treatment of rents from the property. Second, to the extent that any lender making a mortgage loan secured by a multifamily property desires the option to sell the loan later to Fannie Mae, the lender will need to use this form; thus, the form is widely used. Third, unlike the forms that some lenders have created, this form is relatively even-handed and contains many of the points that the borrower's counsel would seek on behalf of her client. Fourth, because the form is a "deed of trust" rather than a "mortgage," it contemplates the potential use of a "power of sale" remedy (a nonjudicial sale of the property after a default that is available in approximately 35 jurisdictions) and thus contains additional provisions relating to this special power. Finally, the form is both comprehensive and up-to-date, containing provisions in response to many of the most current developments in the law and practice of real estate finance. The authors have endeavored to point out deficiencies in any of these respects.

The book is organized around the provisions of the form Deed of Trust. It proceeds with the first substantive section of the Deed of Trust and proceeds through the form on a section-by-section basis. It also includes those sections of the form Note that are referenced in the Deed of Trust. Each section sets forth the verbatim text of a specific provision of the Deed of Trust, immediately followed by commentary on the quoted provision. The commentary explains what the provision means, what functions the provision serves, and any problems with the application or enforcement of the provision from the lender's or borrower's perspective. The commentary includes basic information that any lawyer new to mortgage transactions would find helpful, and provides a thorough analysis that even a lawyer well seasoned in mortgage practice would find useful.

The book can be read cover to cover, especially by someone new to the practice of mortgage transactions. Hopefully, the book will provide useful insight both to lawyers handling their first mortgage transactions and to more seasoned mortgage lawyers looking for a useful reference source.

Definitions

The following terms, when used in this Instrument (including when used in the above recitals), shall have the following meanings:

(a) **"Borrower"** means all persons or entities identified as "Borrower" in the first paragraph of this Instrument, together with their successors and assigns.

(b) **"Collateral Agreement"** means any separate agreement between Borrower and Lender for the purpose of establishing replacement reserves for the Mortgaged Property, establishing a fund to assure completion of repairs or improvements specified in that agreement, or assuring reduction of the outstanding principal balance of the Indebtedness if the occupancy of or income from the Mortgaged Property does not increase to a level specified in that agreement, or any other agreement or agreements between Borrower and Lender which provide for the establishment of any other fund, reserve or account.

(c) **"Environmental Permit"** means any permit, license, or other authorization issued under any Hazardous Materials Law with respect to any activities or businesses conducted on or in relation to the Mortgaged Property.

(d) **"Event of Default"** means the occurrence of any event listed in Section 22.

(e) **"Fixtures"** *means all property which is so attached to the Land or the Improvements as to constitute a fixture under applicable law, including: machinery, equipment, engines, boilers, incinerators, installed building materials; systems and equipment for the purpose of supplying or distributing heating, cooling, electricity, gas, water, air, or light; antennas, cable, wiring and conduits used in connection with radio, television, security, fire prevention, or fire detection or otherwise used to carry electronic signals; telephone systems and equipment; elevators and related machinery and equipment; fire detection, prevention and extinguishing systems and apparatus; security and access control systems and apparatus; plumbing systems; water heaters, ranges, stoves, microwave ovens, refrigerators, dishwashers, garbage disposers, washers, dryers and other appliances; light fixtures, awnings, storm windows and storm doors; pictures, screens, blinds, shades, curtains and curtain rods; mirrors; cabinets, paneling, rugs and floor and wall coverings; fences, trees and plants; swimming pools; and exercise equipment.*

(f) **"Governmental Authority"** *means any board, commission, department or body of any municipal, county, state or federal governmental unit, or any subdivision of any of them, that has or acquires jurisdiction over the Mortgaged Property or the use, operation or improvement of the Mortgaged Property.*

(g) **"Hazardous Materials"** *means petroleum and petroleum products and compounds containing them, including gasoline, diesel fuel and oil; explosives; flammable materials; radioactive materials; polychlorinated biphenyls ("PCBs") and compounds containing them; lead and lead-based paint; asbestos or asbestos-containing materials in any form that is or could become friable; underground or above-ground storage tanks, whether empty or containing any substance; any substance the presence of which on the Mortgaged Property is prohibited by any federal, state or local authority; any substance that requires special handling; and any other material or substance now or in the future defined as a "hazardous substance," "hazardous material," "hazardous waste," "toxic substance," "toxic pollutant," "contaminant," or "pollutant" within the meaning of any Hazardous Materials Law.*

(h) **"Hazardous Materials Laws"** *means all federal, state, and local laws, ordinances and regulations and standards, rules, policies and other governmental requirements, administrative rulings and court judgments and decrees in effect now or in the future and including all amendments, that relate to Hazardous Materials and apply to Borrower or to the Mortgaged Property. Hazardous Materials Laws include, but are not limited to, the*

Comprehensive Environmental Response, Compensation and Liability Act, 42 U.S.C. Section 9601, et seq., the Resource Conservation and Recovery Act, 42 U.S.C. Section 6901, et seq., the Toxic Substance Control Act, 15 U.S.C. Section 2601, et seq., the Clean Water Act, 33 U.S.C. Section 1251, et seq., and the Hazardous Materials Transportation Act, 49 U.S.C. Section 5101, et seq., and their state analogs.

(i) **"Impositions"** and **"Imposition Deposits"** are defined in Section 7(a).

(j) **"Improvements"** means the buildings, structures, improvements, and alterations now constructed or at any time in the future constructed or placed upon the Land, including any future replacements and additions.

(k) **"Indebtedness"** means the principal of, interest on, and all other amounts due at any time under, the Note, this Instrument or any other Loan Document, including prepayment premiums, late charges, default interest, and advances as provided in Section 12 to protect the security of this Instrument.

(l) [Intentionally omitted]

(m) **"Key Principal"** means the natural person(s) or entity identified as such at the foot of this Instrument, and any person or entity who becomes a Key Principal after the date of this Instrument and is identified as such in an amendment or supplement to this Instrument.

(n) **"Land"** means the land described in Exhibit A.

(o) **"Leases"** means all present and future leases, subleases, licenses, concessions or grants or other possessory interests now or hereafter in force, whether oral or written, covering or affecting the Mortgaged Property, or any portion of the Mortgaged Property (including proprietary leases or occupancy agreements if Borrower is a cooperative housing corporation), and all modifications, extensions or renewals.

(p) **"Lender"** means the entity identified as "Lender" in the first paragraph of this Instrument and its successors and assigns, or any subsequent holder of the Note.

(q) **"Loan Documents"** means the Note, this Instrument, all guaranties, all indemnity agreements, all Collateral Agreements, O&M Programs, and any other documents now or in the future executed by Borrower, Key Principal, any guarantor or any other person in connection with the loan evidenced by the Note, as such documents may be amended from time to time.

(r) **"Loan Servicer"** means the entity that from time to time is designated by Lender to collect payments and deposits and receive notices under the

Note, this Instrument and any other Loan Document, and otherwise to service the loan evidenced by the Note for the benefit of Lender. Unless Borrower receives notice to the contrary, the Loan Servicer is the entity identified as "Lender" in the first paragraph of this Instrument.

(s) **"Mortgaged Property"** means all of Borrower's present and future right, title and interest in and to all of the following:

(1) the Land;

(2) the Improvements;

(3) the Fixtures;

(4) the Personalty;

(5) all current and future rights, including air rights, development rights, zoning rights and other similar rights or interests, easements, tenements, rights-of-way, strips and gores of land, streets, alleys, roads, sewer rights, waters, watercourses, and appurtenances related to or benefitting the Land or the Improvements, or both, and all rights-of-way, streets, alleys and roads which may have been or may in the future be vacated;

(6) all proceeds paid or to be paid by any insurer of the Land, the Improvements, the Fixtures, the Personalty or any other part of the Mortgaged Property, whether or not Borrower obtained the insurance pursuant to Lender's requirement;

(7) all awards, payments and other compensation made or to be made by any municipal, state or federal authority with respect to the Land, the Improvements, the Fixtures, the Personalty or any other part of the Mortgaged Property, including any awards or settlements resulting from condemnation proceedings or the total or partial taking of the Land, the Improvements, the Fixtures, the Personalty or any other part of the Mortgaged Property under the power of eminent domain or otherwise and including any conveyance in lieu thereof;

(8) all contracts, options and other agreements for the sale of the Land, the Improvements, the Fixtures, the Personalty or any other part of the Mortgaged Property entered into by Borrower now or in the future, including cash or securities deposited to secure performance by parties of their obligations;

(9) all proceeds from the conversion, voluntary or involuntary, of any of the above into cash or liquidated claims, and the right to collect such proceeds;

(10) all Rents and Leases;

(11) all earnings, royalties, accounts receivable, issues and profits from the Land, the Improvements or any other part of the Mortgaged Property, and all undisbursed proceeds of the loan secured by this Instrument and, if Borrower is a cooperative housing corporation, maintenance charges or assessments payable by shareholders or residents;

(12) all Imposition Deposits;

(13) all refunds or rebates of Impositions by any municipal, state or federal authority or insurance company (other than refunds applicable to periods before the real property tax year in which this Instrument is dated);

(14) all tenant security deposits which have not been forfeited by any tenant under any Lease; and

(15) all names under or by which any of the above Mortgaged Property may be operated or known, and all trademarks, trade names, and goodwill relating to any of the Mortgaged Property.

(t) **"Note"** means the Multifamily Note described on page 1 of this Instrument, including the Acknowledgment and Agreement of Key Principal to Personal Liability for Exceptions to Non-Recourse Liability (if any), and all schedules, riders, allonges and addenda, as such Multifamily Note may be amended from time to time.

(u) **"O&M Program"** is defined in Section 18(a).

(v) **"Personalty"** means all furniture, furnishings, equipment, machinery, building materials, appliances, goods, supplies, tools, books, records (whether in written or electronic form), computer equipment (hardware and software) and other tangible personal property (other than Fixtures) which are used now or in the future in connection with the ownership, management or operation of the Land or the Improvements or are located on the Land or in the Improvements, and any operating agreements relating to the Land or the Improvements, and any surveys, plans and specifications and contracts for architectural, engineering and construction services relating to the Land or the Improvements and all other intangible property and rights relating to the operation of, or used in connection with, the Land or the Improvements, including all governmental permits relating to any activities on the Land.

(w) **"Property Jurisdiction"** is defined in Section 30(a).

(x) **"Rents"** means all rents (whether from residential or non-residential space), revenues and other income of the Land or the Improvements, including parking fees, laundry and vending machine income and fees and *charges for food, health care and other services provided at the Mortgaged Property, whether now due, past due, or to become due, and deposits forfeited by tenants.*

(y) **"Taxes"** *means all taxes, assessments, vault rentals and other charges, if any, general, special or otherwise, including all assessments for schools, public betterments and general or local improvements, which are levied, assessed or imposed by any public authority or quasi-public authority, and which, if not paid, will become a lien, on the Land or the Improvements.*

(z) **"Transfer"** *means (A) a sale, assignment, transfer or other disposition (whether voluntary, involuntary or by operation of law); (B) the granting, creating or attachment of a lien, encumbrance or security interest (whether voluntary, involuntary or by operation of law); (C) the issuance or other creation of an ownership interest in a legal entity, including a partnership interest, interest in a limited liability company or corporate stock; (D) the withdrawal, retirement, removal or involuntary resignation of a partner in a partnership or a member or manager in a limited liability company; or (E) the merger, dissolution, liquidation, or consolidation of a legal entity. "Transfer" does not include (i) a conveyance of the Mortgaged Property at a judicial or non-judicial foreclosure sale under this Instrument or (ii) the Mortgaged Property becoming part of a bankruptcy estate by operation of law under the United States Bankruptcy Code. For purposes of defining the term "Transfer," the term "partnership" shall mean a general partnership, a limited partnership, a joint venture and a limited liability partnership, and the term "partner" shall mean a general partner, a limited partner and a joint venturer.*

Explanation

The foregoing definitions are discussed, where appropriate, in the succeeding sections of the book.

Uniform Commercial Code Security Agreement

This Instrument is also a security agreement under the Uniform Commercial Code for any of the Mortgaged Property which, under applicable law, may be subject to a security interest under the Uniform Commercial Code, whether acquired now or in the future, and all products and cash and non-cash proceeds thereof (collectively, **"UCC Collateral"**), and Borrower hereby grants to Lender a security interest in the UCC Collateral. Borrower shall execute and deliver to Lender, upon Lender's request, financing statements, continuation statements and amendments, in such form as Lender may require to perfect or continue the perfection of this security interest. Borrower shall pay all filing costs and all costs and expenses of any record searches for financing statements that Lender may require. Without the prior written consent of Lender, Borrower shall not create or permit to exist any other lien or security interest in any of the UCC Collateral. If an Event of Default has occurred and is continuing, Lender shall have the remedies of a secured party under the Uniform Commercial Code, in addition to all remedies provided by this Instrument or existing under applicable law. In exercising any remedies, Lender may exercise its remedies against the UCC Collateral separately or together, and in any order, without in any way affecting the availability of Lender's other remedies. This Instrument constitutes a financing statement with respect to any part of the Mortgaged Property which is or may become a Fixture.

Explanation

Every income-producing real estate development includes some personal property. Most obviously, there is usually some tangible property, such as equipment (lawn-mowing, pool-cleaning, computers, etc.) and furniture (office desks, chairs, etc.). Less obviously, the proceeds of some operations on the premises may be personal property. Under traditional common-law thinking, rents from real property are also real property themselves. However, not all proceeds arising from a real estate project are rents in the technical sense. The characterization of the proceeds may be ambiguous. Among the types of revenue that have been controversial are hotel room "rentals," receipts from the "rental" of boat slips, nursing home revenues, golf course greens fees, parking lot receipts, student dormitory "rents," and auto raceway ticket sales.

The Restatement (Third) of Property: Mortgages § 4.2 (1997) adopts a broad definition of rents: "Rents means the proceeds payable by a lessee, licensee, or other person for the right to possess, use, or occupy the real property of another." However, there is no assurance that all state courts will adopt the Restatement's position. *See* R. Wilson Freyermuth, *Of Hotel Revenues, Rents, and Formalism in the Bankruptcy Courts: Implications for Reforming Commercial Real Estate*, 40 UCLA L. REV. 1461 (1993). The Bankruptcy Reform Act of 1994, Pub. L. No. 103-394, enlarged the scope of "rents" as cash collateral under Bankruptcy Code § 363(a) to include "the fees, charges, accounts or other payments for the use or occupancy of rooms and other public facilities in hotels, motels, or other lodging properties." But this definition is not binding outside the bankruptcy context.

For these reasons, mortgage lenders invariably obtain from their borrowers a security agreement under U.C.C. Article 9 covering the personal property associated with the project. Some lenders prefer to employ a separate document as the security agreement, but in the case of the present form it is built into the real estate mortgage.

To perfect the lender's security interest in personal property, it is generally necessary to file a financing statement. Mortgage lenders therefore routinely obtain and file such a statement in the appropriate county or state office. However, a different sort of filing is necessary with respect to fixtures, that is, articles of personal property that are attached to the real estate with the intent that they become a permanent part of it. Under U.C.C. § 9-501(a)(1), a "fixture filing" must be made "in the office designated for the filing or recording of a record of a mortgage on the related real property"—typically a county recorder's office. Paragraph 2 provides that the Deed of Trust itself constitutes a financing statement with respect to fixtures, so that recording of the Deed of Trust will accomplish the "fixture filing."

Assignment of Rents; Appointment of Receiver; Lender in Possession

section 3

(a) As part of the consideration for the Indebtedness, Borrower absolutely and unconditionally assigns and transfers to Lender all Rents. It is the intention of Borrower to establish a present, absolute and irrevocable transfer and assignment to Lender of all Rents and to authorize and empower Lender to collect and receive all Rents without the necessity of further action on the part of Borrower. Promptly upon request by Lender, Borrower agrees to execute and deliver such further assignments as Lender may from time to time require. Borrower and Lender intend this assignment of Rents to be immediately effective and to constitute an absolute present assignment and not an assignment for additional security only. For purposes of giving effect to this absolute assignment of Rents, and for no other purpose, Rents shall not be deemed to be a part of the **"Mortgaged Property,"** as that term is defined in Section 1(s). However, if this present, absolute and unconditional assignment of Rents is not enforceable by its terms under the laws of the Property Jurisdiction, then the Rents shall be included as a part of the Mortgaged Property and it is the intention of the Borrower that in this circumstance this Instrument create and perfect a lien on Rents in favor of Lender, which lien shall be effective as of the date of this Instrument.

Explanation

Reasons for taking an assignment of rents. Lenders would not bother to take assignments of rents if foreclosure were always swift and certain. However, state law foreclosure proceedings may take from a few months to a year or more, with lengthy periods especially common in urban areas of states that still require foreclosure by judicial action. In addition, borrowers often file bankruptcy when faced with impending foreclosure. Even in a Chapter 7 liquidation bankruptcy, the "automatic stay" will probably delay foreclosure for a number of months; in a Chapter 11 reorganization, the delay may be even longer.

During the period between default and foreclosure, the borrower is unlikely to make any debt service payments. Hence, the accrual of interest on the loan will cause its balance to increase. At the same time, the borrower may "milk" the property, deferring maintenance expenses, taxes, and other operating costs while capturing the entire rental cash flow. Thus, the property's value may be declining at the same time the loan balance is rising. Property that was adequate security for the loan when the default occurred may quickly become inadequate in these circumstances.

The lender's chief remedy for this problem is to attempt to capture the rental cash flow and apply it toward operating expenses and debt service. Even if the cash flow is inadequate to meet the full debt service, capturing it will prevent "milking" and make some contribution toward the accruing interest. *See* Julia Patterson Forrester, *A Uniform and More Rational Approach to Rents as Security for the Mortgage Loan*, 46 RUTGERS L. REV. 349 (1993).

Why is the assignment absolute in form? An assignment of rents can be expressed in at least three different ways. First, it could, by its terms, be an assignment "as additional security" for the mortgage debt. This might be termed a "collateral assignment," since the rents would be described as collateral in addition to, and distinct from, the real property itself. Under Restatement (Third) of Property: Mortgages § 4.2 (1997), this sort of assignment is referred to as a "mortgage on the rents." The clause, in simplified form, might read as follows:

> Mortgagor hereby grants to mortgagee a security interest in the rents, issues, and profits paid by tenants in the property. Upon default in the payment of the indebtedness secured hereby, the mortgagee may, at its option, either with or without taking possession of the property, collect all rents, issues, and profits paid by tenants in

the property and apply them toward the indebtedness secured hereby.

Second, the assignment could be a *true* "absolute" assignment, in which the lender *immediately* begins collecting the rents from the inception of the loan. Sometimes a bank "lockbox" arrangement is used in such assignments, with the tenants paying their rents into the lockbox and the lender having exclusive access to it. Of course, most borrowers strongly resist such an absolute assignment, since it means they must give up control of the rents from the outset. A lockbox arrangement is sometimes employed as part of a "workout" on a defaulted loan, but it is not common to see it implemented in an original loan agreement, except in loans on income-producing real estate that are going into a pool to be securitized.

The third type of rents assignment is the type represented in the Fannie Mae subsection reproduced above, and is the type nearly always employed in modern mortgages on income-producing properties. The assignment is described in "absolute" terms, as in subsection (a) above, but the borrower is granted a "license" to collect the rents until a default occurs, as in subsection (b) below. Thus, before default, the borrower is expected to pay the debt service and operating expenses, but may retain any excess cash flow. This sort of assignment is sometimes described as "conditionally absolute," since the arising of a condition of default triggers actual enforcement by the lender.

For all practical purposes, it is obvious that this third and most common type of rents assignment is, like the first kind described above, a collateral or security assignment or, as the Restatement puts it, a "mortgage on the rents." To say, as does subsection (a) of the Deed of Trust, that the assignment is a "present, absolute and irrevocable transfer," when in the next breath the borrower is given the right to collect the rents until default, is a transparent sham. Courts have often recognized this fact. "The fact that the assignments are conditioned upon default and will terminate upon satisfaction of the debt indicates that they are merely additional security for the loan and not an absolute transfer of the Debtor's interest in the rents." *In re* Lyons, 193 B.R. 637 (Bankr. D. Mass. 1996). Yet this sham is found in virtually all modern mortgages.

What does the lender expect to accomplish by using "absolute assignment" language to describe what is plainly a security assignment? There are several objectives. The first derives from the state law rule, widely followed, that requires a lender to take some "affirmative action" to enforce a security assignment of rents. The states vary as to what action is required, but typical examples include the mortgagee's taking direct possession of the property, getting a receiver appointed, or obtaining a court order sequestering the rents for the mortgagee's benefit. *See, e.g.,* Oryx Energy Co. v. Union Nat'l Bank, 895 S.W.2d 368 (Tex. Ct. App. 1995); Comerica Bank-Illinois v. Harris Bank, 673 N.E.2d 380 (Ill. App. Ct. 1996); Galleria Towers, Inc. v. Crump Warren & Sommer, Inc., 831 P.2d 908 (Colo. Ct. App. 1991); *In re* Raleigh/Spring Forest Apartment Ass'n, 118 B.R. 42 (Bankr. E.D.N.C. 1990). Some states are a bit more liberal, requiring the lender only to notify the borrower. *See In re* Fluge, 57 B.R. 451 (Bankr. D.N.D. 1985); CAL. CIV. CODE § 2938 (1996); RESTATEMENT (THIRD) OF PROPERTY: MORTGAGES § 4.2 (1997).

But whatever affirmative action is required, it will inevitably be somewhat time-consuming, and any delay means that some rents will be lost to the lender. By using the "absolute assignment" language instead, the lender hopes that courts will treat the "affirmative action" requirement as inapplicable, and will recognize the lender's right to all rents paid after the date of default. Sometimes this argument works; *see, e.g.,* Credit Lyonnais v. Getty Square Associates, 876 F.Supp. 517 (S.D.N.Y. 1995). Many state courts, however, regard this approach with skepticism; *see* Oryx Energy Co. v. Union Nat'l Bank, 895 S.W.2d 368 (Tex. Ct. App. 1995). For that reason, the concluding sentence of subsection (a) of the Deed of Trust concedes that if under state law the assignment is not regarded as absolute, it will nonetheless be effective to create a security interest—a mortgage or lien on the rents.

Rents in bankruptcy. When the owner of rental real estate files bankruptcy, all of his or her nonexempt assets become the property of the trustee in bankruptcy (or, in a Chapter 11 proceeding, the debtor-in-possession (DIP), who has all of the powers of a bankruptcy trustee). Because a mortgage lender's ability to obtain the rents from the trustee or DIP is problematic (as discussed below), the lender who has used a "conditionally absolute" assignment-of-rents clause may simply argue that the rents had been transferred to the lender before the bankruptcy petition was filed, and hence never came into the hands of the trustee or DIP. As noted above, this is an unrealistic and somewhat silly view of the "conditionally absolute" assignment, but it has prevailed in a few cases, mainly in states following the "title theory" of mortgages. *See, e.g.,* Commerce Bank v. Mountain View Village Inc., 5 F.3d 34 (3d Cir.1993); *In re* Galvin, 120 B.R. 767, 770–72 (Bankr. D. Vt. 1990); Jason Realty, L.P. v. First Fidelity Bank, 59 F.3d 423 (3rd Cir. 1995) (New Jersey law). This result is more likely to be reached if the lender has taken some pre-petition steps, such as obtaining a receiver or actually intercepting the rents, to enforce the rents clause.

Most bankruptcy courts, however, have rejected this view and concluded that the rents remain assets of the debtor despite the presence of a "conditionally absolute" assignment. *See In re* Guardian Realty Group, L.L.C., 205 B.R. 1, 3 (Bankr. D. Colo. 1997); Lyons v. Federal Savings Bank, 193 B.R. 637, 649 (Bankr. D. Mass. 1996); *In re* 5028 Wisconsin Avenue Associates Ltd. Partnership, 167 B.R. 699, 704–05 (Bankr. D.D.C. 1994); *In re* Willows of Coventry Ltd. Partnership, 154 B.R. 959 (Bankr. N.D. Ind. 1993); *In re* Foundry of Barrington Oaks Partnership, 129 B.R. 550 (Bankr. N.D. Ill. 1991) ("[The creditor] can call this arrangement an 'absolute assignment' or, more appropriately, 'Mickey Mouse.' It's still a lien, and the rent is still the debtor's property, subject to that lien").

Perfection of the assignment of rents.   A number of bankruptcy cases in the late 1980s and early 1990s confused the concepts of "perfection" and "enforcement" of assignments of rents. They held that a security interest in rents was not *perfected* until the taking of the "affirmative action" required by state law (e.g., appointment of a receiver, a court order sequestering the rents, or the taking of possession by the mortgagee). They seemed not to realize that these acts were required for *enforcement* of the security interest, not for its *perfection*, and that perfection was accomplished simply by recording the assignment of rents. Hence, they held that a trustee in bankruptcy or DIP could assume the role of a perfected lien creditor under the "strong arm" powers of Bankruptcy Code § 544 and set aside the assignment of rents. *See, e.g., In re* Bond, 122 B.R. 39 (D. Md. 1990). Lenders concluded that this result was much less probable if they used a "conditionally absolute" form of assignment than if they employed a "security assignment." This provided an additional rationale for lenders to use "conditionally absolute" assignments.

This unfortunate episode is now ended. During the latter part of the 1990s, the vast majority of bankruptcy court decisions have recognized that *perfection* of an assignment of rents (whether of the "security assignment" or the "conditionally absolute" type) is accomplished simply by recording it. *See, e.g., In re* Fairview-Takoma Ltd. Partnership, 206 B.R. 792 (D. Md. 1997). In addition, a number of states have recently enacted statutes providing that recording constitutes perfection. Thus, this reason for using a "conditionally absolute" form of assignment has lost much of its significance.

Rents as cash collateral.   If the rents are still the debtor's property, an undersecured mortgage lender may nonetheless get control of them (or "adequate protection" in lieu of them) if they are recognized as "cash collateral" by the bankruptcy court under Bankruptcy Code § 363(a). It is clear that, in general, cash collateral includes rents. Section 363(a) provides that

> "cash collateral" means, cash . . . or other cash equivalents when-ever acquired in which the estate and an entity other than the es-tate have an interest and includes the proceeds, products, offspring, rents, or profits of property subject to a security interest as provided in section 552(b) of this title, whether existing before or after the commencement of a case under this title.

Ordinarily, under § 552 a pre-petition lien will not cover "after-acquired property," that is, property the debtor receives after the bankruptcy petition is filed. However, rents are different from other after-acquired property. Section 552(b) recognizes the effectiveness of a *pre*-petition security agreement to govern *post*-petition rents "to the extent provided in [the] security agreement." Prior to the Bankruptcy Reform Act of 1994, § 552(b) included an additional phrase after that just quoted: "and by applicable nonbankruptcy law." Lenders generally believed that using a "conditionally absolute" assignment of rents would help them convince the bankruptcy courts that their security interests in rents were cognizable under state law, and hence met the last-quoted stan-dard. The 1994 act deleted the reference to nonbankruptcy law and, in the view of some commentators, federalized the law with respect to va-lidity of assignments of rents as governing post-petition rents. Whether this is so is unclear; *see* R. Wilson Freyermuth, *The Circus Continues— Security Interests in Rents, Congress, the Bankruptcy Courts, and the "Rents Are Subsumed in the Land" Hypothesis*, 6 J. BANKR. LAW & PRAC. 115 (1997). Thus, use of a "conditionally absolute" form of assignment may still strengthen the lender's argument for treating post-petition rents as cash collateral.

(b) *After the occurrence of an Event of Default, Borrower authorizes Lender to collect, sue for and compromise Rents and directs each tenant of the Mortgaged Property to pay all Rents to, or as directed by, Lender. However, until the occurrence of an Event of Default, Lender hereby grants to Borrower a revocable license to collect and receive all Rents, to hold all Rents in trust for the benefit of Lender and to apply all Rents to pay the installments of interest and principal then due and payable under the Note and the other amounts then due and payable under the other Loan Documents, including Imposition Deposits, and to pay the current costs and expenses of managing, operating and maintaining the Mortgaged Property, including utilities, Taxes and insurance premiums (to the extent not included in Imposition Deposits), tenant improvements and other capital expenditures. So long as no Event of Default has occurred and is continuing, the Rents remaining after application pursuant to the preceding sentence may be retained by Borrower free and clear of, and released from, Lender's rights with respect to Rents under this Instrument. From and after the occurrence of an Event of Default, and without the necessity of Lender entering upon and taking and maintaining control of the Mortgaged Property directly, or by a receiver, Borrower's license to collect Rents shall automatically terminate and Lender shall without notice be entitled to all Rents as they become due and payable, including Rents then due and unpaid. Borrower shall pay to Lender upon demand all rents to which Lender is entitled. At any time on or after the date of Lender's demand for Rents, Lender may give, and Borrower hereby irrevocably authorizes Lender to give, notice to all tenants of the Mortgaged Property instructing them to pay all Rents to Lender, no tenant shall be obligated to inquire further as to the occurrence or continuance of an Event of Default, and no tenant shall be obligated to pay to Borrower any amounts which are actually paid to tender in response to such a notice. Any such notice by Lender shall be delivered to each tenant personally, by mail or by delivering such demand to each rental unit. Borrower shall not interfere with and shall cooperate with Lender's collection of such Rents.*

Explanation

Notifying tenants. Whatever the law says about how to enforce an assignment of rents, it is clear that as a practical matter, when a default occurs the tenants must be notified and instructed to pay rent to the lender. In many cases, there is no assurance that the tenants will cooperate. Paragraph 3(b) of the Deed of Trust authorizes the lender to send a notice to the tenants, and makes it clear that the tenants are justified in paying rent directly to the lender. However, some tenants may find the notice confusing or annoying, and may simply refuse to pay anybody until faced with a court order.

Some lenders use an additional technique to make the transition work more smoothly. They require the borrower to prepare and execute letters to the tenants, advising them to begin paying their rents to the lender. These letters are held by the lender "in escrow" until default, and are then mailed or delivered to the tenants. Of course, this approach is not foolproof; each time a new lease is entered into, the borrower must sign a new letter and put it in the lender's hands. In a multifamily apartment project this is probably impractical, but it may make sense in a loan on an office building or shopping center, in which there are fewer leases and their terms are much longer.

A tenant will be protected in continuing to pay rent directly to the landlord until the tenant is notified that the assignment of rents is being enforced. *See* RESTATEMENT (SECOND) OF CONTRACTS § 338.

(c) *Borrower represents and warrants to Lender that Borrower has not executed any prior assignment of Rents (other than an assignment of Rents securing indebtedness that will be paid off and discharged with the proceeds of the loan evidenced by the Note), that Borrower has not performed, and Borrower covenants and agrees that it will not perform, any acts and has not executed, and shall not execute, any instrument which would prevent Lender from exercising its rights under this Section 3, and that at the time of execution of this Instrument there has been no anticipation or prepayment of any Rents for more than two months prior to the due dates of such Rents. Borrower shall not collect or accept payment of any Rents more than two months prior to the due dates of such Rents.*

Explanation

Conflicting assignments of rents. Rents are a property right distinct from the real estate itself. Assignments of rents are conveyances of interests in real property, and presumably subject to the recording acts. Hence, if the borrower had made a previous assignment of rents, but it was unrecorded, the lender who had no notice of it and recorded its own mortgage with an assignment of rents would take priority over the previous, unrecorded assignment. The covenant by the borrower that no competing assignment of rents has been executed is simply designed to give the lender a bit of extra comfort on this point.

Incidentally, the same priority principles govern appointment of receivers. Hence, a receiver appointed at the request of the holder of a senior mortgage will supplant a receiver appointed at the request of a junior mortgage holder. *See* RESTATEMENT (THIRD) OF PROPERTY: MORTGAGES § 4.5 (1997).

Prepaid rents. A landlord who recognizes that foreclosure and loss of the building are inevitable may be tempted to "milk" the property by collecting prepaid rents from the tenants for many months in the future, often at a large discount. Paragraph 3(c) of the Deed of Trust limits the landlord to collection of two months' worth of advance rent, but there is no way for the lender to ensure that the landlord will comply with this limitation. If the landlord enters into an agreement with a tenant that is not "commercially reasonable," a subsequently appointed receiver may disaffirm it. *See* RESTATEMENT (THIRD) OF PROPERTY: MORTGAGES § 4.4 (1997). Accepting prepaid rent at a large discount would probably be regarded as "commercially unreasonable"; *see* New York City Community Preservation Corp. v. Michelin Ass'n, 496 N.Y.S.2d 530 (App. Div. 1985). However, if rent were prepaid at the normal rental rate or something close to it, it is doubtful that a receiver would be permitted to disaffirm it; *see* Chemical Bank v. Evans & Hughes Realty, 613 N.Y.S.2d 239 (N.Y. App. Div. 1994).

(d) *If an Event of Default has occurred and is continuing, Lender may, regardless of the adequacy of Lender's security or the solvency of Borrower and even in the absence of waste, enter upon and take and maintain full control of the Mortgaged Property in order to perform all acts that Lender in its discretion determines to be necessary or desirable for the operation and maintenance of the Mortgaged Property, including the execution, cancellation or modification of Leases, the collection of all Rents, the making of repairs to the Mortgaged Property and the execution or termination of contracts providing for the management, operation or maintenance of the Mortgaged Property, for the purposes of enforcing the assignment of Rents pursuant to Section 3(a), protecting the Mortgaged Property or the security of this Instrument, or for such other purposes as Lender in its discretion may deem necessary or desirable. Alternatively, if an Event of Default has occurred and is continuing, regardless of the adequacy of Lender's security, without regard to Borrower's solvency and without the necessity of giving prior notice (oral or written) to Borrower, Lender may apply to any court having jurisdiction for the appointment of a receiver for the Mortgaged Property to take any or all of the actions set forth in the preceding sentence. If Lender elects to seek the appointment of a receiver for the Mortgaged Property at any time after an Event of Default has occurred and is continuing, Borrower, by its execution of this Instrument, expressly consents to the appointment of such receiver, including the appointment of a receiver ex parte if permitted by applicable law. Lender or the receiver, as the case may be, shall be entitled to receive a reasonable fee for managing the Mortgaged Property. Immediately upon appointment of a receiver or immediately upon the Lender's entering upon and taking possession and control of the Mortgaged Property, Borrower shall surrender possession of the Mortgaged Property to Lender or the receiver, as the case may be, and shall deliver to Lender or the receiver, as the case may be, all documents,*

records (including records on electronic or magnetic media), accounts, sur-
veys, plans, and specifications relating to the Mortgaged Property and all
security deposits and prepaid Rents. In the event Lender takes possession
and control of the Mortgaged Property, Lender may exclude Borrower and
its representatives from the Mortgaged Property. Borrower acknowledges
and agrees that the exercise by Lender of any of the rights conferred under
this Section 3 shall not be construed to make Lender a mortgagee-in-pos-
session of the Mortgaged Property so long as Lender has not itself entered
into actual possession of the Land and Improvements.

Explanation

Becoming a mortgagee-in-possession.   This section identifies two specific
mechanisms for enforcement of the assignment of rents. The first allows the
lender to take possession of the mortgaged property, and the second authorizes the appointment of a receiver to take possession and operate the
mortgaged property. These mechanisms are not the lender's exclusive remedies, because in most states the lender could begin collecting rent, or could
get a court order forcing the borrower to turn over all collected rents to the
lender, without either taking possession or obtaining a receiver.

Even without mortgage language that authorizes the mortgagee to
take possession, in a title theory or intermediate theory state a mortgagee may take possession as soon as a default occurs. In lien theory
states, however, the mortgagee may take possession only when the
mortgagor has abandoned the property or gives consent to the mortgagee's taking of possession. In effect, paragraph 3(d) of the Deed of
Trust constitutes a pre-default consent.

However, if the property is located in a lien theory state, this advance consent may not be enforced; *see* RESTATEMENT (THIRD) OF
PROPERTY: MORTGAGES § 4.1(b); WASH. REV. STAT. § 7.28.230, *construed
in In re* Federal Shopping Way, Inc., 457 F.2d 176 (9th Cir. 1972). A few
lien theory states have statutes or case law that does recognize consent
clauses like this. But in most lien theory states, the mortgagee will need
to show abandonment of the property or contemporaneous consent by
the mortgagor at the time the mortgagee takes possession. Nevertheless,
even in states that generally refuse to enforce language like that of paragraph 3(d), it does no harm, and might conceivably convince a judge in
an individual case to give the mortgagee possession.

Risks of mortgagee-in-possession status.   In most cases, the lender
will prefer to get a receiver appointed rather than taking direct posses-

sion. The reason is that there are extreme risks to a mortgagee who takes possession prior to foreclosure. Such a mortgagee is held to a very high standard of conduct in managing the property. *See* G. NELSON & D. WHITMAN, REAL ESTATE FINANCE LAW § 4.24ff (3d ed. 1993). Liabilities imposed on the mortgagee include:

a. Strict accounting for all rents and other revenues collected, with duties to the mortgagor that are tantamount to fiduciary in nature; *see* Johns v. Moore, 336 P.2d 579 (Cal. Ct. App. 1959). These duties may be asserted by the mortgagor or by junior lienholders; *see* Shadow Lawn Savings & Loan Ass'n v. Palmarozza, 463 A.2d 384 (N.J. Super. App. Div. 1983). The mortgagee is entitled to apply rent receipts to repairs, taxes, and other necessary operating expenses. *See* Gomez v. Bobker, 508 N.Y.S.2d 215 (App. Div. 1986); Herman v. Herman, 707 P.2d 1374 (Wash. Ct. App. 1985); Martinez v. Continental Enterprises, 697 P.2d 789 (Colo. App. 1984).

b. A duty to manage the property in a reasonable, prudent, and careful manner; use reasonable means to prevent damage to it; and keep it productive. *See* ComFed Savings Bank v. Newtown Commons Plaza Ass'n, 719 F. Supp. 367 (E.D. Pa. 1989).

c. Liability in tort to third parties injured on the premises. *See* City of Newark v. Sue Corp., 304 A.2d 567 (N.J. Super. 1973). *Cf.* Briglia v. Mondrian Mortgage Corp., 698 A.2d 28 (N.J. Super. 1997) (mortgagee in possession not a "commercial landlord" for purposes of sidewalk maintenance ordinance). *See also* Central Heights Condominium Ass'n, Inc. v. Little Falls Savings & Loan Ass'n, 598 A.2d 233 (N.J. Super. 1991) (mortgagee in possession who completed construction of condominiums liable to unit purchasers for construction defects); Castillo v. Carver Federal Savings & Loan Ass'n, 508 N.Y.S.2d 574 (App. Div. 1986) (mortgagee in possession could be liable for injuries due to fire on premises if causation were shown).

d. Liability under statutes imposing duties on owners. *See, e.g.,* Hausman v. City of Dayton, 1993 WL 541649 (Ohio App. 1993) (duty to clean up asbestos contamination); Craig v. Mohyde, 1997 WL 206630 (Conn. Super. 1997) (duty to residential tenants to make repairs under a residential landlord-tenant statute).

e. Liability for all goods and services furnished by third parties to the property. *See* Essex Cleaning Contractors, Inc. v. Amato, 317 A.2d 411 (N.J. Super. 1974).

f.   Liability for breach of any covenants running with the land, or covenants running with the ground leasehold estate if the project is built on a ground lease. *See* U.S. Fidelity and Guardian Co. v. Old Orchard Plaza Ltd. Partnership, 672 N.E.2d 876 (Ill. Ct. App. 1996); Moffatt v. Smith, 4 N.Y. 1145 (1850); Cockrell v. Houston Packing Co., 147 S.W. 1145 (1912). This includes the duty to make repairs at the behest of tenants if the lease so provides; *see* Touma v. St. Mary's Bank, 712 A.2d 619 (N.H. 1998).

Few lenders have staff members well qualified to carry out these duties, and fewer still are willing to accept the associated liabilities. Employing a receivership instead avoids the liabilities, and if the receiver is a professional rental property manager, he or she will probably do a better job than the lender would do. Receiverships have one additional advantage: They do not terminate subordinate leases, while the taking of possession by the mortgagee arguably will do so, at least in title theory states. In a residential rental project, the possibility of terminating subordinate leases unwittingly is not likely to be a major concern. However, in a commercial building it can be a serious problem, and provides another reason that receiverships are generally preferable to direct possession by the mortgagee. *See* HRPT Advisors, Inc. v. MacDonald, Levine, Jenkins & Co., P.C., 686 N.E.2d 203 (Mass Ct. App. 1997) (mortgagee's taking of possession will not terminate junior leases if mortgagee does so in its capacity as assignee of rents rather than its capacity as a foreclosing lender).

A lender does not become a mortgagee-in-possession merely by collecting the rents, unless the lender also takes physical possession and begins operating the property. *See* Prince v. Brown, 856 P.2d 589 (Okla. Ct. App. 1993). Nonetheless, it is all too easy for a mortgagee to take possession unwittingly. For example, the lender who enters into a new lease with a tenant is almost surely "in possession." *See* Skolnick v. East Boston Savings Bank, 29 N.E.2d 585, 130 A.L.R. 1519 (1940). A lender who undertakes to evict a tenant for nonpayment of rent, or makes repairs at the request of a tenant, may well be considered to have taken possession. *Cf.* Blackstone Valley National Bank v. Hanson, 445 N.E.2d 1093 (Mass. Ct. App. 1983) (mortgagee who visited the property a few times, asked a tenant to "take care of it," and made emergency repairs was not "in possession"). Cultivating and harvesting a crop on the land is likely to be deemed possession as well; *see* Nelson v. Bowen, 12 P.2d 1083 (Cal. Ct. App. 1932).

Counsel should caution their lender clients about taking actions that will result in possession status. The final sentence of paragraph 3(d) of the Deed of Trust is designed to ward off the argument that the mere presence of a clause allowing the mortgagee to take possession upon default somehow puts the mortgagee in possession automatically.

Receiverships. Because a receiver is an officer of the court, it is not possible for lenders to dictate in absolute terms the conditions upon which a receiver will be appointed. State law varies but typically requires that one or more of the following factors be present before a court will appoint a receiver: (1) a continuing default on the mortgage debt, (2) inadequacy of the property as security, (3) ongoing commission of waste on the property, (4) the mortgagor's insolvency. *See, e.g.,* Dart v. Western Savings & Loan Ass'n, 438 P.2d 407 (Ariz. 1968).

Hence, the language of the Deed of Trust stating that a receiver can be appointed when there is a continuing default "regardless of the adequacy of Lender's security, without regard to Borrower's solvency" may or may not be enforced by the courts. However, it does no harm and may well influence a court to appoint a receiver even if insolvency or inadequacy of the security is missing. *See* Barclays Bank v. Superior Court, 137 Cal. Rptr. 743 (1977) (mortgage language authorizing a receiver creates a prima facie, but rebuttable, showing of entitlement to receiver). Restatement (Third) of Property: Mortgages § 4.3 (1997) may be helpful to mortgagees in this respect, since it specifically approves the appointment of a receiver if a default exists and the mortgage "contains either mortgage on the rents or a provision authorizing appointment of a receiver to take possession and collect rents upon mortgagor default."

Ex parte receiverships. The subsection above provides for ex parte appointment of a receivership if local law so permits. It does in many states. One might ask, "Does such a judicial action violate procedural due process?" The limited case law on the point suggests that it does not—*see* Friedman v. Gerax Realty Associates, 420 N.Y.S.2d 247 (1979); Hartford Fed. Savings & Loan Ass'n v. Tucker, 491 A.2d 1084 (Conn. 1985)—or that the language in the form authorizing ex parte appointment acts as a waiver of the borrower's due process rights—*see* Manufacturers Life Insurance Co. v. Patterson, 554 N.E.2d 134 (Ohio. Ct. App. 1988).

(e) *If Lender enters the Mortgaged Property, Lender shall be liable to account only to Borrower and only for those Rents actually received. Lender shall not be liable to Borrower, anyone claiming under or through Borrower or anyone having an interest in the Mortgaged Property, by reason of any act or omission of Lender under this Section 3, and Borrower hereby releases and discharges Lender from any such liability to the fullest extent permitted by law.*

Explanation

Relief from strict duties.   Ordinarily a mortgagee-in-possession has a duty to use reasonable diligence in leasing the premises and collecting rents. This subsection attempts to relieve the lender to some degree from this duty, but it is unclear whether the courts will enforce it against the borrower. The exculpation of the lender for "any act or omission" is likewise of doubtful enforceability. For example, if the lender in possession created a dangerous condition on the land, and a third party, injured as a result, sued the borrower (who is, after all, still the landowner), it is difficult to imagine that a court would use a clause such as paragraph 3(e) of the Deed of Trust to relieve the lender of liability.

(f) *If the Rents are not sufficient to meet the costs of taking control of and managing the Mortgaged Property and collecting the Rents, any funds expended by Lender for such purposes shall become an additional part of the indebtedness as provided in Section 12.*

Explanation

Expenditures on the property.   In general, mortgage lenders have a common-law right to make necessary expenditures to protect their security, and to add those expenditures to the loan balance. *See* RESTATEMENT (THIRD) OF PROPERTY: MORTGAGES § 2.2 (1997). Because failure to perform reasonable maintenance constitutes waste under the Restatement (§ 4.6), and because lender expenditures to prevent or correct waste are recognized under § 2.2 (*see* § 2.2, Reporters' Note (e)), courts should readily enforce this subsection. *See* Thompson v. Kirsch, 677 P.2d 490 (Idaho Ct. App. 1984) (advances for maintenance could be added to mortgage balance, where mortgage authorized lender to make such advances).

(g) *Any entering upon and taking of control of the Mortgaged Property by Lender or the receiver, as the case may be, and any application of Rents as provided in this Instrument shall not cure or waive any Event of Default or invalidate any other right or remedy of Lender under applicable law or provided for in this Instrument.*

Assignment of Leases; Leases Affecting the Mortgaged Property

(a) As part of the consideration for the Indebtedness, Borrower absolutely and unconditionally assigns and transfers to Lender all of Borrower's right, title and interest in, to and under the Leases, including Borrower's right, power and authority to modify the terms of any such Lease, or extend or terminate any such Lease. It is the intention of Borrower to establish a present, absolute and irrevocable transfer and assignment to Lender of all of Borrower's right, title and interest in, to and under the Leases. Borrower and Lender intend this assignment of the Leases to be immediately effective and to constitute an absolute present assignment and not an assignment for additional security only. For purposes of giving effect to this absolute assignment of the Leases, and for no other purpose, the Leases shall not be deemed to be a part of the "Mortgaged Property," as that term is defined in Section I(s). However, if this present, absolute and unconditional assignment of the Leases is not enforceable by its terms under the laws of the Property Jurisdiction, then the Leases shall be included as a part of the Mortgaged Property and it is the intention of the Borrower that in this circumstance this Instrument create and perfect a lien on the Leases in favor of Lender, which lien shall be effective as of the date of this Instrument.

(b) Until Lender gives notice to Borrower of Lender's exercise of its rights under this Section 4, Borrower shall have all rights, power and authority granted to Borrower under any Lease (except as otherwise limited by this

27

Section or any other provision of this Instrument), including the right, power and authority to modify the terms of any Lease or extend or terminate any Lease. Upon the occurrence of an Event of Default, the permission given to Borrower pursuant to the preceding sentence to exercise all rights, power and authority under Leases shall automatically terminate. Borrower shall comply with and observe Borrower's obligations under all Leases, including Borrower's obligations pertaining to the maintenance and disposition of tenant security deposits.

Explanation

Assignments of leases.   Why does the lender want an assignment of *leases* in addition to an assignment of rents? Because the right to rents per se probably will not authorize the lender to modify the terms of a lease, or to extend or terminate a lease. For example, if the lender commences collecting rents under the assignment of rents, and a particular tenant is delinquent, the lender would like to have the power to renegotiate the lease terms in order to help the tenant cure the delinquency, or to terminate the lease if no satisfactory resolution can be achieved. Note that this is far from being a complete authority to manage the property, since it does not permit the lender to enter into new leases with respect to vacant space. To do that, the lender will probably either have to become a mortgagee-in-possession or get a receiver appointed.

The Deed of Trust phrases the assignment of leases in absolute terms for the same reasons discussed above regarding assignments of rents. The statement that the assignment of leases is not "an assignment for additional security only" is as fictitious here as in the assignment of rents, because the lender's power over leases is conditioned upon, and can only be exercised in the event of, a default. Hence, it is in reality a security assignment.

(c) Borrower acknowledges and agrees that the exercise by Lender, either directly or by a receiver, of any of the rights conferred under this Section 4 shall not be construed to make Lender a mortgagee-in-possession of the Mortgaged Property so long as Lender has not itself entered into actual possession of the Land and the Improvements. The acceptance by Lender of the assignment of the Leases pursuant to Section 4(a) shall not at any time or in any event obligate Lender to take any action under this Instrument or to expend any money or to incur any expenses. Lender shall not be liable in any way for any injury or damage to person or property sustained by any person or persons, firm or corporation in or about

the Mortgaged Property. Prior to Lender's actual entry into and taking possession of the Mortgaged Property, Lender shall not (i) be obligated to perform any of the terms, covenants and conditions contained in any Lease (or otherwise have any obligation with respect to any Lease); (ii) be obligated to appear in or defend any action or proceeding relating to the Lease or the Mortgaged Property; or (iii) be responsible for the operation, control, care, management or repair of the Mortgaged Property or any portion of the Mortgaged Property. The execution of this Instrument by Borrower shall constitute conclusive evidence that all responsibility for the operation, control, care, management and repair of the Mortgaged Property is and shall be that of Borrower, prior to such actual entry and taking of possession.

Explanation

Avoiding mortgagee-in-possession status.   Once again the Deed of Trust attempts to give the lender the maximum possible authority over the landlord-tenant relationship without imposing the substantial risks of mortgagee-in-possession status. However, it is unclear (and doubtful) whether a court will take this disclaimer language at face value. While the mere *acceptance* of the assignment of leases probably will not make the lender a mortgagee-in-possession, *exercise* of authority over the leases (e.g., renegotiation of their terms) probably will, whether the lender has physically possessed the property or not. *See* Prince v. Brown, 856 P.2d 589 (Okla. Ct. App. 1993).

Likewise, it is clear that a mortgagee-in-possession is liable for personal injuries to third parties caused by the mortgagee's management activities. *See* Skolnick v. East Boston Savings Bank, 29 N.E.2d 585, 130 A.L.R. 1519 (1940). It is extremely unlikely that a disclaimer of this duty in the mortgage would preclude a court from imposing liability on the mortgagee.

(d) *Upon delivery of notice by Lender to Borrower of Lender's exercise of Lender's rights under this Section 4 at any time after the occurrence of an Event of Default, and without the necessity of Lender entering upon and taking and maintaining control of the Mortgaged Property directly, by a receiver, or by any other manner or proceeding permitted by the laws of the Property Jurisdiction, Lender immediately shall have all rights, powers and authority granted to Borrower under any Lease, including the right, power and authority to modify the terms of any such Lease, or extend or terminate any such Lease.*

(e) Borrower shall, promptly upon Lender's request, deliver to Lender an executed copy of each residential Lease then in effect. All Leases for residential dwelling units shall be on forms approved by Lender, shall be for initial terms of at least six months and not more than two years, and shall not include options to purchase. If customary in the applicable market, residential Leases with terms of less than six months may be permitted with Lender's prior written consent.

Explanation

Lender control of leasing activity.   Lenders have a strong and legitimate interest in the leases their borrowers enter into. The value of a rental building is heavily dependent on the quality of its tenants and their obligations under the leases. In mortgages on retail and office properties, the lender may insist on reviewing and approving each tenant and lease. In residential properties, where there are more tenants and greater turnover, individualized lender review and approval are not practical, so paragraph 3(e) of the Deed of Trust substitutes a requirement that the borrower shall execute leases only on a lender-approved form.

(f) Borrower shall not lease any portion of the Mortgaged Property for non-residential use except with the prior written consent of Lender and Lender's prior written approval of the Lease agreement. Borrower shall not modify the terms of, or extend or terminate, any Lease for non-residential use (including any lease in existence on the date of this Instrument) without the prior written consent of Lender. Borrower shall, without request by Lender, deliver an executed copy of each non-residential Lease to Lender promptly after such Lease is signed. All non-residential Leases, including renewals or extensions of existing Leases, shall specifically provide that (1) such Leases are subordinate to the lien of this Instrument (unless waived in writing by Lender); (2) the tenant shall attorn to Lender and any purchaser at a foreclosure sale, such attornment to be self-executing and effective upon acquisition of title to the Mortgaged Property by any purchaser at a foreclosure sale or by Lender in any manner; (3) the tenant agrees to execute such further evidences of attornment as Lender or any purchaser at a foreclosure sale may from time to time request; (4) the Lease shall not be terminated by foreclosure or any other transfer of the Mortgaged Property; (5) after a foreclosure sale of the Mortgaged Property, Lender or any other purchaser at such foreclosure sale may, at Lender's

or such purchaser's option, accept or terminate such Lease; and (6) the tenant shall, upon receipt after the occurrence of an Event of Default of a written request from Lender, pay all Rents payable under the Lease to Lender.

Explanation

Subordination and attornment of nonresidential tenants. If a project covered by the Deed of Trust includes some commercial (e.g., retail) space, the lender will wish to treat it differently from the residential space. The lender will indeed review and exercise an individualized approval right, and will retain a copy of each lease.

The borrower is required to include in each nonresidential lease two of the three clauses found in a "subordination, nondisturbance, and attornment agreement." The two clauses are the subordination and attornment clauses. Subordination is useful because it allows the foreclosure purchaser to terminate the lease and evict the tenant if the purchaser views the lease as undesirable. Attornment is useful because it allows the foreclosure purchaser, in the same situation, to insist that the tenant remain on the lease if the purchaser views the lease as desirable. In effect, the lender can choose whether to have its cake or eat it. There is, however, no nondisturbance clause protecting the tenant from eviction in the event of foreclosure; indeed, provision (5) expressly provides that the lease may be terminated after foreclosure.

Some commercial tenants, especially those with significant bargaining power, may find the absence of a nondisturbance clause unacceptable. Pressure from such a tenant may force the landlord/borrower to go back to the lender and seek special approval to grant the tenant a nondisturbance covenant.

(g) *Borrower shall not receive or accept Rent under any Lease (whether residential or non-residential) for more than two months in advance.*

Explanation

Prepaid rent. This is simply a recapitulation of the provision in paragraph 3(c) prohibiting the collection of prepaid rent for more than two months. Of course, a borrower who is under severe financial stress may be tempted to "milk" the property by collecting additional prepaid rents notwithstanding this prohibition.

Payment of Indebtedness; Performance under Loan Documents; Prepayment Premium

Borrower shall pay the Indebtedness when due in accordance with the terms of the Note and the other Loan Documents and shall perform, observe and comply with all other provisions of the Note and the other Loan Documents. Borrower shall pay a prepayment premium in connection with certain prepayments of the Indebtedness, including a payment made after Lender's exercise of any right of acceleration of the Indebtedness, as provided in the Note.

Fannie Mae Form Note
Prepayment Provision

10. Voluntary and Involuntary Prepayments

a. A prepayment premium shall be payable in connection with any prepayment made under this Note as provided below:

1. Borrower may voluntarily prepay all (but not less than all) of the unpaid principal balance of this Note on the last Business Day of a calendar month if Borrower has given Lender at least 30 days prior notice of its intention to make such prepayment. Such prepayment shall be made by paying (A) the amount of principal being prepaid, (B) all accrued interest, (C) all other

33

sums due Lender at the time of such prepayment, and (D) the prepayment premium calculated pursuant to Schedule A.   For all purposes, including the accrual of interest, any prepayment received by Lender on any day other than the last calendar day of such month shall be deemed to have been received on the last calendar day of each month. For purposes of this Note, a **"Business Day"** means any day other than a Saturday, Sunday or any other day on which Lender is not open for business.

2.   Upon Lender's exercise of any right of acceleration under this Note, Borrower shall pay to Lender, in addition to the entire un-paid principal balance of this Note outstanding at the time of the acceleration, (A) all accrued interest and all other sums due Lender under this Note and the other Loan Documents, and (B) the prepayment premium calculated pursuant to Schedule A.

3.   Any application by Lender of any collateral or other security to the repayment of any portion of the unpaid principal bal-ance of this Note prior to the Maturity Date and in the ab-sence of acceleration shall be deemed to be a partial prepayment by Borrower, requiring the payment to Lender by Borrower of a prepayment premium. The amount of any such partial prepayment shall be computed so as to provide to Lender a prepayment premium computed pursuant to Schedule A without Borrower having to pay out-of-pocket any additional amounts.

b.   Notwithstanding the provisions of Paragraph 10(a), no prepayment premium shall be payable with respect to (A) any prepayment made no more than 90 days before the Maturity Date, or (B) any prepayment occurring as a result of the application of any insur-ance proceeds or condemnation award under the Security Instrument.

c.   Schedule A is hereby incorporated by reference into this Note.

d.   Any required prepayment of less than the unpaid principal of this Note shall not extend or postpone the due date of any subsequent monthly installments or change the amount of such installments, un-less Lender agrees otherwise in writing.

e.   Borrower recognizes that any prepayment of the unpaid principal balance of this Note, whether voluntary or involuntary or resulting from a default by Borrower, will result in Lender's incurring loss, including reinvestment loss, additional expense and frustration or impairment of Lender's ability to meet its commitments to third parties. Borrower agrees to pay to Lender upon demand damages for the detriment caused by any prepayment, and agrees that it is extremely difficult and impractical to ascertain the extent of such damages. Borrower therefore acknowledges and agrees that the formula for calculating prepayment premiums set forth on Schedule A represents a reasonable estimate of the damages Lender will incur because of a prepayment.

f.   Borrower further acknowledges that the prepayment premium provisions of this Note are a material part of the consideration for the loan evidenced by this Note, and acknowledges that the terms of this Note are in other respects more favorable to Borrower as a result of the Borrower's voluntary agreement to the prepayment provisions.

Schedule A

Prepayment Premium.   Any prepayment payable under Paragraph 10 of this Note shall be computed as follows:

a.   If the prepayment is made during the first _____ years beginning on the date of the Note (the **"Yield Maintenance Period"**), the prepayment premium shall be the greater of:

i.   1% of the unpaid principal balance of this Note; or

ii. The product obtained by multiplying:

   A.   the amount of principal being prepaid,
        by

   B.   the difference obtained by subtracting from the interest rate on this Note the yield rate (the **"Yield Rate"**) on the _____% U.S. Treasury Security due _____ (the **"Specified U.S. Treasury Security"**), as the Yield Rate is reported in *The Wall Street Journal* on the fifth Business Day preceding (x) the date notice of prepayment is given to Lender where prepayment is voluntary, or (y) the date Lender accelerates the Loan,
        by

   C.   the present value factor calculated using the following formula:

$$\frac{1 - (1 + r)^{-n}}{r}$$

[r = Yield Rate

n = the number of 365-day years (or 366-day years, if applicable), and any fraction thereof, remaining between the Prepayment Date and the expiration of the Yield Maintenance Period]

In the event that no Yield Rate is published for the Specified U.S. Treasury Security, then the nearest equivalent U.S. Treasury Security shall be selected at Lender's discretion. If the publication of such Yield Rates in *The Wall Street Journal* is discontinued, Lender shall determine such Yield Rates from another source selected by Lender.

For purposes of subparagraph (ii)(C), the **"Prepayment Date"** shall be (x) in the case of a voluntary prepayment, the date on which the prepayment is made, and (y) in any other case, the date on which Lender accelerates the unpaid principal balance of this Note.

b. If the prepayment is made after the expiration of the Yield Maintenance Period but more than 90 days before the Maturity Date, the prepayment premium shall be 1% of the unpaid principal balance of this Note.

INITIAL(S)

Explanation

Conditions for prepayment of the loan.   Paragraph 5 of the Deed of Trust addresses the "guts" of the loan transaction: that the borrower pay the debt and perform the other obligations imposed by the loan documents in accordance with the terms of the loan documents. Most real estate secured loans are long-term loans (a construction loan is the primary example of a short-term loan). Most of these long-term loans accrue interest at a fixed rate (e.g., 8 percent per annum) as opposed to a floating rate (e.g., "prime" plus 1 percent). If interest rates rise during the term of the loan, a lender would not have the right to demand that the borrower pay off the indebtedness immediately so that the lender could reinvest the loan proceeds in a higher-interest-rate loan. This is because the typical loan documents provide for monthly payment of interest and some amortization of principal with the balance, if any, due at the maturity of the loan. For the same reason, most courts have ruled that if interest rates have dropped during the term of the loan, a borrower is not entitled to prepay the loan in order to enjoy a new loan at a lower rate of interest. This is known as the "perfect tender in time" rule. If the loan documents are structured in the way described above, and are "silent" on the issue of prepayment, then the majority of courts will apply the "perfect tender in time" rule and not permit the borrower to prepay the debt. See Frank S. Alexander, *Mortgage Prepayment: The Trial of Common Sense*, 72 CORNELL L. REV. 288 (1987); Debra P. Stark, *New Developments in Enforcing Prepayment Charges*, 26 REAL PROP. PROB. & TR. J. 213 (1991). However, a growing minority of jurisdictions would allow the borrower to prepay the debt if the loan documents are silent on the issue. See John C. Murray, *Enforceability of Prepayment Premium Provisions in Commercial Loan Documents, in* COMMERCIAL REAL ESTATE FINANCING (PLI Handbook 1999).

Most loan documents are not silent on the issue of prepayment. The Fannie Mae Form Note permits complete prepayment of the loan if the borrower pays to the lender a prepayment premium to compensate the lender for the losses that it will or may incur in connection with the prepayment (the potential reinvestment loss described above and other losses and expenses that the lender may incur). The Form Note provides that no prepayment charge will be imposed in the event of a casualty or condemnation when insurance proceeds or the condemnation award are applied to the debt (in these two instances the prepayment is beyond the control and fault of the borrower, and many lenders have opted not to require a charge in that context), or when a prepayment is made within 90 days before the stated maturity date of the loan (this gives the borrower a window period to obtain and close on a refinancing). The Form Note clarifies that the prepayment charge applies whether the prepayment is "voluntary" or "involuntary" (i.e., a default by the borrower and acceleration of the debt by the lender).

Addressing "involuntary" prepayments. It is important that the loan documents clarify that a prepayment charge will apply in an "involuntary" prepayment situation; when loan documents have failed to clarify this, courts have refused to enforce the prepayment charges when the borrower has defaulted and the lender has accelerated the debt. See, *e.g.*, Slevin Container Corp. v. Provident Federal Savings & Loan

Ass'n, 424 N.E. 2d 939 (Ill. App. Ct. 1981); *In re* LHD Realty Corp., 726 F.2d 327 (7th Cir. 1984). However, when loan documents clearly require a prepayment charge in a default/acceleration situation, courts have enforced the imposition of such charges. *See, e.g.,* Pacific Trust Co. TTEE v. Fidelity Federal Savings & Loan Ass'n, 184 Cal. App. 3d 817, 824, 229 Cal. Rptr. 269, 274 (1986); Village of Rosemont v. Maywood-Proviso State Bank, 149 Ill. App. 3d 1087, 501 N.E. 2d 859 (1986); Eyde v. Empire of American Federal Savings Bank, 701 F. Supp. 126 (E.D. Mich. 1988).

Methods for calculating prepayment charges.   The second major issue is how to calculate the prepayment charge. Older loan documents provided for a charge based upon a specified percentage multiplied against the balance of the loan being paid off (e.g., 10 percent). Typically, the percentage would decline as the loan became closer to maturing (the idea being that as the loan got closer to maturing, the lender's damages from prepayment declined). This method was obviously imprecise (e.g., if interest rates had actually risen, then the lender would have no pure reinvestment losses; conversely, if interest rates had dropped significantly, it is possible that the lender would suffer losses in excess of 10 percent of the balance of the loan). Due to this imprecision, and the need to more accurately guarantee that the yields to maturity in the loan documents be maintained even if the loans were paid off early, lenders began to use a "yield maintenance formula" to calculate the prepayment charge.

Schedule A of the Form Note provides for a yield maintenance formula. Under this formula, one multiplies the principal amount being prepaid by the difference between the interest rate on the note and the yield rate on a specified U.S. Treasury security at the time of the attempted prepayment or acceleration of the loan. The theory behind this comparison is that upon repayment of the debt, the lender can reinvest the amount paid with the purchase of the U.S. Treasury security. If the U.S. Treasury security is accruing interest at the same or a higher interest rate than under the note, then the lender suffers no lost opportunity cost as a result of the prepayment, and thus no charge is owed. If the U.S. Treasury security is accruing interest at a lower interest rate than under the note, the borrower must pay a prepayment charge equal to that difference in rates multiplied by the balance of the loan to compensate the lender for that difference. Under the terms of the Form Note, this amount is then discounted to its present value (to account for the fact that receiving the money today is worth more than receiving the money 10 years from now). It should be noted, however, that the calculation of the prepayment charge in the Form Note provides for the greater of 1 percent of the unpaid balance of the loan or the difference in interest rates described above. Consequently, even if interest rates have risen since the loan was made, at least a 1 percent charge would apply. It should also be noted that under the Form Note, the yield maintenance formula applies only to a set number of years of the loan (it is a blank in the form). Once that period expires up to 90 days before the stated maturity, only a 1 percent charge would apply. This is obviously a very important blank to fill in, and presumably relates to a date after which the lender is no longer as concerned with preserving the yield under the loan.

Enforcing prepayment charges. There are hundreds of reported cases involving the enforcement of prepayment charges. Most current litigation over prepayment charges focuses upon either the manner in which they are calculated or challenges that they are unenforceable, either as a "penalty" under a liquidated-damages analysis or because they are "unreasonable" under Bankruptcy Code section § 506(b). Some courts, usually bankruptcy courts, have applied a liquidated-damages analysis to the charge and have ruled that the yield maintenance formula is an unreasonable estimate of the loss a lender will suffer. These courts point out that because U.S. Treasury securities are a safer investment than first real estate mortgage loans, the Treasury rate will be lower than the mortgage loan rate when the loan is first made. As a result, these courts have concluded, it is unreasonable to compare U.S. Treasury security yields with the interest rate under the first mortgage loan and that such comparison gives the lender more than it originally bargained for. See In re Skyler Ridge, 80 B.R. 500 (Bankr. C.D. Cal. 1987); In re Kroh Bros. Dev. Co., 88 B.R. 997 (Bankr. W.D. Md. 1988). Instead, the U.S. Treasury security yield should be upwardly adjusted to reflect the higher rate then being offered for first mortgage loans. Lenders counter that they may no longer be in the real estate mortgage lending business at the time the borrower prepays the debt, and so they will not be reinvesting the loan proceeds in this manner. Lenders also argue that even if they are still in the mortgage lending business, it is difficult if not impossible to find a truly comparable real estate mortgage loan, so the lender will suffer a loss if it must upwardly adjust its formula in this fashion. Some courts accept the lenders' arguments on this issue See, e.g., New England Mutual Life Insurance Co. v. Stuzin, No. 86-2740-S, 86-2471-S, 1990 WL 25, 2171 (D. Mass. 1990); R-D Investment Co. v. Mutual Benefit Life Insurance Co., No. 880-883 (Dist. Ct. Neb. Sept. 19, 1991).

There is also a split of authority on enforcement of a prepayment charge based on a specified percentage. Prior to the *Skyler Ridge* decision, courts exercised very little scrutiny of the amount of the charge, and enforced charges of between 5 and 50 percent of the outstanding balance of the loan. *See, e.g.,* Northway Lanes v. Hackley Union National Bank & Trust Co., 334 F. Supp. 723 (W.D. Mich. 1971), *aff'd,* 464 F. 2d 855 (6th Cir. 1972); Williams v. Fassler, 110 Cal App. 3d 7, 12, 167 Cal. Rptr. 545, 548 (1980). In these cases the courts viewed the prepayment charge as the bargained-for consideration for the privilege of prepayment. But when courts have applied a liquidated-damages analysis, there is a split of authority on the outcomes. One court enforced a prepayment charge of 10 percent even when applying a liquidated-damages analysis; *see In re* Schaumburg Hotel Owner Ltd. Partnership, 97 B.R. 943 (Bankr. N.D. Ill. 1989). Another court indicated that a charge of 10 percent takes on the characteristics of a penalty; *see* Clinton Capital Corp. v. Straeb, 589 A.2d 1363, 1371 (N.J. Super. 1990). Yet another court held that even a charge of 1 percent is unreasonable since it presumed a reinvestment loss; *see In re* A.J. Lane and Co., Inc., 113 B.R. 821 (Bankr. D. Mass. 1990).

It is fairly safe to conclude that in a non-default situation, a court would and should enforce the prepayment charge in the note as the bargained-for consideration for the privilege of prepayment. As a practice point, it helps if the note in fact uses this type of language (or language similar to that appearing in paragraph 10(f) of the Form Note) in the "voluntary prepayment" section. In a default situation, however, the prepayment charge used in the note is susceptible to challenge as an unreasonable penalty applying a liquidated-damages analysis, depending upon the precedent that the court is bound to follow or that the court finds persuasive. The provision does not upwardly adjust the Treasury security to reflect the higher first mortgage interest rate. In addition, it provides for a minimum 1 percent fee, which presumes a loss in all cases (even those cases in which no reinvestment yield loss actually results).

Following are a few additional suggestions to increase the likelihood of enforcement of the prepayment charge in light of the case law in this area. First, because some courts analyze whether the charge is reasonable in light of the actual losses the lender has suffered, it is very important when enforcing the prepayment charge to provide the court with adequate evidence of the extent of the lender's harm. If the lender can show that the actual losses equal or exceed the charge, then the court is more likely to enforce the charge. It is also a good idea to provide an example of how the prepayment charge would be calculated so that the borrower will be less likely to assert that it did not really understand the provision. This type of argument arose in cases when prepayment charges using "yield maintenance formulas" equaled as much as 30 percent of the loan amount being paid off. Had an example reflected the possibility of such a high charge, this would support the argument that the borrower knew what it was agreeing to. Lenders can also require reasoned opinions on the enforceability of the charge and provide for springing liability if the borrower (or related person or entity) challenges its enforcement (which may reduce the likelihood of a challenge). One should also have the borrower acknowledge in the loan documents why Treasury yields were being used (that the lender might not be making mortgage loans and the difficulty of finding a comparable mortgage loan to reinvest the prepaid money in) and why there is a minimum 1 percent charge (e.g., identify the other costs and losses of the lender due to the prepayment that are separate from the issue of a loss in yield upon reinvestment).

Exculpation

Borrower's personal liability for payment of the Indebtedness and for performance of the other obligations to be performed by it under this Instrument is limited in the manner, and to the extent, provided in the Note.

Fannie Mae Form Note
Exculpation Provision

9.   Limits on Personal Liability

a.   Except as otherwise provided in this Paragraph 9, Borrower shall have no personal liability under this Note, the Security Instrument or any other Loan Document for the repayment of the Indebtedness or for the performance of any other obligations of Borrower under the Loan Documents, and Lender's only recourse for the satisfaction of the Indebtedness and the performance of such obligations shall be Lender's exercise of its rights and remedies with respect to the Mortgaged Property and any other collateral held by Lender as security for the Indebtedness. This limitation on Borrower's liability shall not limit or impair Lender's enforcement of its rights against any guarantor of the Indebtedness or any guarantor of any obligations of Borrower.

b.   Borrower shall be personally liable to Lender for the repayment of a portion of the Indebtedness equal to any loss or damage suffered by Lender as a result of (1) failure of Borrower to pay to Lender upon demand after an Event of Default, all Rents to which Lender is entitled under Section 3(a) of the Security Instrument and the amount of all security deposits collected by Borrower from tenants then in residence; (2) failure of Borrower to apply all insurance proceeds and condemnation proceeds as required by the Security Instrument; (3) failure of Borrower to comply with Section 14(d) or (e) of the Security Instrument relating to the delivery of books and records, statements, schedules and reports; (4) fraud or written material misrepresentation by Borrower, Key Principal or any officer, director, partner, member or employee of Borrower in connection with the application for or creation of the Indebtedness or any request for any action or consent by Lender; or (5) failure to apply Rents, first, to the payment of reasonable operating expenses (other than Property management fees that are not currently payable pursuant to the terms of an Assignment of Management Agreement or any other agreement with Lender executed in connection with the Loan) and then to amounts (**"Debt Service Amounts"**) payable under this Note, the Security Instrument or any other Loan Document (except that Borrower will not be personally liable (i) to the extent that Borrower lacks the legal right to direct the disbursement of such sums because of a bankruptcy, receivership or similar judicial proceeding, or (ii) with respect to Rents that are distributed in any calendar year if Borrower has paid all operating expenses and Debt Service Amounts for that calendar year).

c.   Borrower shall become personally liable to Lender for the repayment of all of the Indebtedness upon the occurrence of any of the following Events of Default: (1) Borrower's acquisition of any property or operation of any business not permitted by Section 33 of the Security Instrument; or (2) a Transfer that is an Event of Default under Section 21 of the Security Instrument.

d.   To the extent that Borrower has personal liability under this Paragraph 9, Lender may exercise its rights against Borrower personally without regard to whether Lender has exercised any rights against the Mortgaged Property or any other security, or pursued any rights against any guarantor, or pursued any other rights available to Lender under this Note, the Security Instrument, any other Loan Document or applicable law. For purposes of this Paragraph 9, the term **"Mortgaged Property"** shall not include any funds that (1) have been applied by Borrower as required or permitted by the Security Instrument prior to the occurrence of an Event of Default, or (2) Borrower was unable to apply as required or permitted by the Security Instrument because of a bankruptcy, receivership, or similar judicial proceeding.

Explanation

The development of "carve-outs" to nonrecourse loans.   Prior to the 1990s, lenders typically made long-term commercial real estate loans on a "nonrecourse" basis (the property mortgaged was the sole asset the lender could look to in the event that the borrower defaulted in performing its obligations under the loan documents). Lenders were willing to make nonrecourse loans to real estate projects that were fully constructed and profitably operating, loaning typically up to 80 percent of the appraised value of the property. In the event of a default, the lender could accelerate the debt, foreclose on the property, and recover its investment.

During the real estate recession of the early 1990s, numerous real estate projects began to fail and numerous real estate loans went into default. Lenders learned many lessons as they attempted to enforce the loan contracts they had entered into. One common problem lenders encountered was borrowers who would "milk" the mortgaged property (i.e., take income from the property and not apply it to the expenses of the property). The borrowers might be applying that money to other projects that the lender did not have a mortgage on, or purchasing other assets that the lender did not have a security interest in, or developing a "war chest" to fund a defense to the lender's foreclosure action (in particular, filing for bankruptcy relief). In reaction, lenders have since revised their loan documentation to provide "carve-outs" to the nonrecourse nature of the loan (conditions that will cause the borrower to become personally liable to the lender for repayment of a portion of the debt equal to the loss or damage suffered by the lender as a result of the circumstance).

Articulating specific carve-outs versus general carve-outs.   Paragraph 9(a) of the Form Note provides for the basic nonrecourse nature of the loan. Paragraph 9(b) contains the carve-outs to the nonrecourse nature of the loan, including, the borrower's misapplication of rents, insurance proceeds, or condemnation proceeds, or fraud or written material misrepresentation by the borrower. Paragraph 9(c) provides that the borrower becomes personally liable for the entire debt if (i) the borrower changes its status as a "single asset borrower" (by mixing in additional properties, the borrower increases the possibility that it could be subject to a bankruptcy filing—a possibility that secured lenders assiduously seek to avoid) or (ii) the borrower makes a prohibited transfer of the mortgaged property or of the borrowing entity under paragraph 21 of the Deed of Trust. These carve-outs could prove very useful to lenders that in the past had carve-outs only for "waste" or "fraud" attached to their nonrecourse loans.

The Restatement (Third) of Property: Mortgages § 4.6(3) provides that "[w]aste occurs when, without the mortgagee's consent, the mortgagor . . . fails to pay before delinquency property taxes or governmental assessments secured by a lien having priority over the mortgage." To the extent that future court decisions rely upon the Restatement position, a nonrecourse lender whose loan documents contain a carve-out for waste should be able to establish a claim in cases where the borrower has failed to pay real estate taxes. Nevertheless, pre-Restatement case law reflects a split of authority on whether failure to pay taxes constitutes "waste," and in a number of reported decisions courts have denied lenders recovery under nonrecourse loans. For example, in *Chetek State Bank v. Barberg*, 489 N.W.2d 385 (Wis. Ct. App. 1992), various lenders (hereinafter "Bank") held a collective commercial mortgage on appellants' property. The mortgage and note contained nonrecourse language absolving the various mortgagors (general partners and companies) of any personal liability to Bank on any money judgment with no "carve-outs." The mortgage subsequently went into default, and the property was sold at a sheriff's sale that resulted in a deficiency of over $1 million. Bank's complaint in the foreclosure contained a cause of action alleging tortious waste as a result of the appellants' failure to pay real estate taxes and interest on the note, as the mortgage required. The circuit court granted a default judgment against appellant Barberg and summary judgment against appellant Stucky in the amount of the unpaid taxes and interest, holding that nonpayment of taxes and interest constituted tortious waste that rendered them liable notwithstanding the nonrecourse language. The appellate court reversed, stating that the nonpayment of interest and taxes did not constitute tortious waste. The court stated that tortious waste required unreasonable conduct by the possessor of the property that results in physical damage to the property and substantially diminishes its value. The court held that the appellants' failure to pay the taxes and interest was not per se unreasonable conduct, and that the nonpayment did not cause physical damage to the land.

Even when the loan documents provide for a carve-out for "fraud" or "waste," some courts have refused to find liability. *See* FGH Realty Credit Corp. v. Bonati, 641 N.Y.S.2d 12 (App. Div. 1996) (court held that nonpayment of real estate taxes by mortgagor did not constitute fraud within the meaning of exception to nonrecourse provision in mortgage).

Other courts have embraced the position expressed in the Restatement and have allowed nonrecourse lenders to pursue waste claims in cases involving unpaid taxes. *See* Travelers Insurance Co. v. 633 Third Associates, 973 F.2d 82 (2d. Cir. 1992), *on remand*, 14 F.3d 114 (2d Cir. 1994) (permitting lender to sue mortgagor for waste under nonrecourse loan containing carve-outs for fraud or waste, but noting contrary case law). In *Travelers*, the plaintiff (Travelers), loaned $145 million to defendant (Associates), secured by a mortgage on an office building in New York City. Associates defaulted on the loan and Travelers foreclosed on the property. In addition, Associates had not paid the taxes on the property, resulting in a tax lien. The note and mortgage contained an exculpation clause that stated, in part,

> [N]otwithstanding anything to the contrary contained in this Note or the Mortgage, the liability and obligation of the Exculpated Parties to perform and observe and make good the obligations contained in this Note and the Mortgage shall not be enforced by any action or proceeding wherein damages or any money judgment shall be sought against any of the Exculpated Parties, except a foreclosure action against the Mortgaged Property.

Travelers sued and asked the court to set aside a $4 million cash distribution by the defendant to its two partners as a fraudulent conveyance under the New York Debt and Credit Law §§ 270–281 (McKinney 1990) and to enjoin such future conveyances. The district court held that because the loan was nonrecourse, the plaintiff had no entitlement to the transferred money and therefore the conveyance could not have caused Travelers' injury. Travelers appealed, and the Second Circuit held that while the exculpation clause barred "a tort action seeking money damages for waste of the secured property," it did not bar "an equitable action to prevent waste." 973 F.2d at 85. The court then concluded that New York courts would find that willful nonpayment of property taxes constituted waste and justified equitable relief. *Id.* at 86. The court stated that "the plaintiff may nonetheless have standing under New York's Fraudulent Conveyance Act to set aside the conveyance if the conveyance caused a diminution in the value of the real property, to which plaintiff is entitled to look in the event of default." *Id.* The court remanded the case and granted the plaintiff leave to amend the complaint to assert the claim for equitable relief.

On remand, Travelers filed an amended complaint that included a claim for equitable relief from waste and for specific performance of Associates' obligations, in addition to its original claims for equitable relief from distributions the defendants made to its partners under the law of fraudulent conveyances. The district court dismissed the entire amended complaint, stating that because the court had appointed a receiver for the property, Travelers was no longer in possession, and an equitable action for waste would apply only to a mortgagor-in-possession. The court also added that it was not persuaded that New York law would recognize a willful failure to pay property taxes as waste. The Second Circuit again reversed the district court on both grounds. The court stated that New York courts recognized two general categories of waste: an action against one in control of property who allows the property to deteriorate and decrease in value, and an action by a mortgagee against a mortgagor who impairs the mortgage. 14 F.3d at 120. The court then cited *Union Mortgage Co. v. Nelson*, 275 A.D. 1028 (N.Y. App. Div. 1949), in which the court suggested that the second category for waste may exist where "failure to pay taxes . . . occurred in violation of the mortgagor's obligations or where the failure was willful, intentional, fraudulent, or the like." *Id.* at 122. Consequently, the Second Circuit held that under New York law, waste occurred where the mortgagor fraudulently failed to pay taxes or intentionally failed to pay despite an obligation to do so. *Id.* at 123. The court did qualify its holding, however, stating that not every failure to follow the loan obligations would constitute waste. The court reiterated that the mortgagor's conduct must be fraudulent or intentional and that it must impair the mortgage. *Id.* The court found that the intentional nonpayment of taxes would impair the mortgage because it required the mortgagee to pay the tax lien and any accrued interest before obtaining clear title to the property. The court also defined a willful nonpayment of taxes to be any failure to pay by the mortgagor who is presumed to have knowledge of such taxes and their prior lien status as against the mortgage lien.

These cases underscore the need to be more specific in designating carve-outs than just using the terms "fraud" or "waste," if the mortgagee wants to preserve the right to recover against the personal assets of a borrower when the borrower fails to apply income from the property to the property's expenses. If there is no carve-out language at all, and a lender sues on a tort theory of waste, some courts will not allow the lender to recover without a showing of physical damage. *See Chetek State Bank, supra.* Even with a carve-out for fraud, some courts will not consider the nonpayment of real estate taxes as fraud. *See FGH Realty Credit Corp., supra.* Finally, even the most favorable decision on this issue—*Travelers Insurance Company, supra*—noted that the mortgagee could not maintain an action against the mortgagor with respect to rents that a receiver had handled (apparently, the receiver had mistakenly paid $4 million to the partnership instead of toward the real estate taxes).

Because the Deed of Trust more specifically and clearly explains the situations in which the nonrecourse loan will become a recourse loan, lenders using this form stand a far better chance of recovering against the borrower's personal assets when the borrower fails to apply the income from the property to the expenses of the property. Under this language, the lender should not have to show impairment of the mortgage, fraud, or the elements of tortious waste.

Deposits for Taxes, Insurance and Other Charges

(a) Borrower shall deposit with Lender on the day monthly installments of principal or interest, or both, are due under the Note (or on another day designated in writing by Lender), until the Indebtedness is paid in full, an additional amount sufficient to accumulate with Lender the entire sum required to pay, when due (1) any water and sewer charges which, if not paid, may result in a lien on all or any part of the Mortgaged Property, (2) the premiums for fire and other hazard insurance, rent loss insurance and such other insurance as Lender may require under Section 19, (3) Taxes, and (4) amounts for other charges and expenses which Lender at any time reasonably deems necessary to protect the Mortgaged Property, to prevent the imposition of liens on the Mortgaged Property, or otherwise to protect Lender's interests, all as reasonably estimated from time to time by Lender. The amounts deposited under the preceding sentence are collectively referred to in this Instrument as the **"Imposition Deposits."** The obligations of Borrower for which the Imposition Deposits are required are collectively referred to in this Instrument as **"Impositions."** The amount of the Imposition Deposits shall be sufficient to enable Lender to pay each Imposition before the last date upon which such payment may be made without any penalty or interest charge being added. Lender shall maintain records indicating how much of the monthly Imposition Deposits and how much of the aggregate Imposition Deposits held by Lender are held for the purpose of paying Taxes, insurance pre-

51

miums and each other obligation of Borrower for which Imposition Deposits are required. Any waiver by Lender of the requirement that Borrower remit Imposition Deposits to Lender may be revoked by Lender, in Lender's discretion, at any time upon notice to Borrower.

Explanation

Why do lenders collect escrows?   Paragraph 7(a) of the Deed of Trust allows the lender to collect monthly deposits for a wide variety of items, including (1) lienable water charges against the property, (2) lienable sewer charges against the property, (3) insurance, (4) taxes, and (5) amounts the lender deems necessary to protect the property. The item that lenders most commonly escrow for is taxes, because nonpayment of real estate taxes can result in the taxing authority obtaining a lien on the property that primes the lien of the mortgage. If the borrower does not pay the taxes, the lender will have to pay them in order to protect its investment. Furthermore, because real estate taxes are frequently a large property expense that is payable infrequently (such as annually or semi-annually), requiring a monthly escrow for those items imposes cash flow discipline on the borrower.

Which escrows might the lender waive?   Lenders will frequently negotiate the collection of any type of escrow, even for real estate taxes and insurance. Different lenders place different levels of importance on the maintenance of tax and insurance escrow accounts. For example, it is common for a lender to agree to require that these items be escrowed only after the occurrence of an event of default. The bottom line for the borrower is to ask about the lender's policy. The borrower cannot know if the lender will waive a tax or insurance escrow unless it asks. In contrast, water and sewer charges do not often result in the water or sewer authorities having the ability to impose priming liens on the property. Moreover, these charges are typically payable frequently, such as monthly or quarterly. Thus, there is often less justification for the lender to insist on an escrow for water or sewer charges. Note that under paragraph 7(a) of the Deed of Trust, the lender's ability to require an escrow for "amounts lender deems necessary to protect the property" is very broad. This could include a capital improvements fund or repair items. The lender could decide that new roofs, air conditioning units, signage, or windows are in order. This provision does not require that nonpayment of any escrowed items results in a priming lien. The borrower is well advised to ask the lender to reduce or more strictly define this broad escrow power.

(b) *Imposition Deposits shall be held in an institution (which may be Lender, if Lender is such an institution) whose deposits or accounts are insured or guaranteed by a federal agency. Lender shall not be obligated to open additional accounts or deposit Imposition Deposits in additional institutions when the amount of the Imposition Deposits exceeds the maximum amount of the federal deposit insurance or guaranty. Lender shall apply the Imposition Deposits to pay Impositions so long as no Event of Default has occurred and is continuing. Unless applicable law requires, Lender shall not be required to pay Borrower any interest, earnings or profits on the Imposition Deposits. Borrower hereby pledges and grants to Lender a security interest in the Imposition Deposits as additional security for all of Borrower's obligations under this Instrument and the other Loan Documents. Any amounts deposited with Lender under this Section 7 shall not be trust funds, nor shall they operate to reduce the Indebtedness, unless applied by Lender for that purpose under Section 7(e).*

Explanation

Deposit insurance. Paragraph 7(b) of the Deed of Trust requires escrows to be deposited in an institution insured or guaranteed by a federal agency. The provision does not necessarily mean the Federal Deposit Insurance Corporation. The paragraph also does not explicitly require that the amount on deposit in the escrow account be within the limit of insurance provided by the federal agency. Nor does it require that the account be a segregated account for the benefit of the borrower.

Does the lender have to pay escrow expenses on time? Paragraph 7(b) of the Deed of Trust obligates the lender to apply the imposition deposits to the expenses for which the lender is escrowing. However, it does not require the lender to pay on time. For example, in many states real estate taxes are payable annually by December 31 each year and if they are timely paid, the borrower will have a sizable income tax deduction by reason of payment. Under this section, the lender is not promising to get the borrower her income tax deduction on time. In contrast, under 82 U.S.C. § 2605(g), residential mortgage loan services are required to make payments from escrow accounts for "taxes, insurance premiums, and other charges in a timely manner as such payments become due."

Interest on escrowed money. The Deed of Trust, like most deeds of trust, provides that the lender is not obligated to pay any interest on escrow deposits unless it is required by law to do so. Most states do not require interest on escrow funds.

Perfection of a security interest in money in a deposit account. Paragraph 7(b) of the Deed of Trust also provides that the borrower grants the lender a security interest in the escrowed monies. This grant of a security interest does not mean that the lender necessarily has a perfected security interest in the imposition deposit in the account. Where the lender is a depository institution, retention of the imposition deposit will likely be in a deposit account with the lender. If the lender is not a depository institution, the imposition deposit will be in a deposit account at another financial institution.

Under its 1972 model version, in existence in most states until July 2001, Article 9 does not apply to the creation or perfection of a security interest in a deposit account. U.C.C. § 9-104(1). Under this approach, the lender cannot perfect a security interest in the imposition deposit account merely by filing a financing statement covering the account or by attempting to take "possession" of the account.[1] The 1972 version of Article 9, however, does allow the creation and perfection of a security interest in specific funds within a deposit account where those funds constitute "proceeds" of some other form of Article 9 collateral. U.C.C. §§ 9-104(1), 9-306(2) (security interest in collateral continues in any "identifiable proceeds"). This provision allows the possibility of a priority dispute with regard to the imposition deposits. The lender is going to put the imposition deposits in an account that will be under the exclusive control of the lender, whether the lender is a depository bank or not. The borrower will not be making any deposits on its own into the

---

[1] One might argue under the 1972 version of Article 9 that the funds in the imposition deposit account could be "money"— in which the secured party could perfect a security interest by possession under U.C.C. § 9-305—and not a "deposit account." Some courts have had difficulty distinguishing between "money" and a "deposit account." If the lender is a depository institution, it could be deemed to have possession of money. For example, in In re Gemini at Dadeland, Ltd., 24 B.R.57 (Bankr. S.D. Fla. 1982), a bank took a security interest in a bank account maintained at the bank. The bankruptcy court held that the funds were perfected by possession. Note, however, that the rationale of Gemini effectively takes the deposit account exclusion out of Article 9. In addition, if the lender is not a depository institution and deposits the impositions with a bank, the lender may not be deemed to have possession under Article 9—although possession of Article 9 collateral by an escrow agent is usually deemed to be sufficient possession by the secured party to perfect a security interest. In re O.P.M. Leasing Services, Inc., 46 B.R. 661 (Bankr. S.D.N.Y. 1985).

account, and the borrower will have no independent ability to make withdrawals from the account. Nonetheless, the source of the money paid to the lender and deposited by the lender into the account could be identifiable proceeds from some other secured party's collateral—with that other secured party maintaining a security interest in that money. This means that although a mortgage lender may not be able to obtain an Article 9 perfected security interest in the imposition deposit, another secured party with a lien on proceeds may (if it can meet its tracing burden) be able to reach the imposition deposit account ahead of the mortgage lender.

Even under the 1972 version of Article 9, some states have adopted nonuniform provisions that permit attachment and perfection of a security interest in a deposit account. For example, California provides that a secured party may perfect a security interest in a deposit account by giving written notification of its interest to the depositary bank. Illinois law provides that a security interest in a deposit account is perfected when the security agreement is executed as to deposit accounts maintained with the secured party; as to deposit accounts maintained with any organization other than the secured party, perfection occurs when notice thereof is given in writing to the organization, and that organization provides written acknowledgment of and consent to the notice of the secured party. 810 ILL. COMP. STAT. 5/9-302(1)(i).

Under revised Article 9—now adopted in a majority of states and scheduled to become effective July 1, 2001—there is no longer any exclusion of deposit accounts from the universe of permitted Article 9 collateral. Revised Article 9 permits the creation of a security interest in a deposit account and provides that the secured party may perfect that interest by obtaining (and maintaining) "control" over the deposit account. U.C.C. § 9-314(a) (1999). The secured party has control if

> (1) the secured party is the bank with which the deposit account is maintained; (2) the debtor, secured party and bank have agreed in an authenticated record that the bank will comply with instructions originated by the secured party directing disposition of the funds in the deposit account without further consent by the debtor; or (3) the secured party becomes the bank's customer with respect to the deposit account [U.C.C. § 9-104(a) (1999)].

A secured party that has established control in one of these fashions continues to have control "even if the debtor retains the right to direct the disposition of funds from the deposit account." U.C.C. § 9-104(b) (1999).

Another possibility where the lender is a depositary institution is for the lender to claim a legal right to the imposition deposit by exercise of a right of setoff. Setoff is not a creature of the U.C.C., but rather exists under common law. Setoff prevents parties having to maintain separate litigation that could result in one party having to pay while the other does not. Many courts interpreting the 1972 version of Article 9, however, have concluded that a setoff right is subordinate to the security interest of a competing creditor with a perfected security interest in Article 9 collateral and proceeds. For example, in *Citizens National Bank v. Mid-States Development Co.*, 380 N.E.2d 1243 (Ind. Ct. App. 1978), a secured party traced the proceeds of a perfected security interest into a bank account and asserted priority over the bank's right of setoff. The Indiana Court of Appeals held that Article 9 controlled over the bank's setoff right. Under revised Article 9, a bank's setoff right will be effective, notwithstanding a conflicting "proceeds" security interest in funds within that deposit account, unless the conflicting secured party has become the bank's customer on that deposit account. U.C.C. § 9-340 (1999).

For a thorough discussion of the pre-revised Article 9 rules governing this issue, *see* Gerald T. McLaughlin, *Security Interests in Deposit Accounts: Unresolved Problems and Unanswered Questions Under Existing Law*, 54 BROOKLYN L. REV. 45 (Spring 1988); and Alvin C. Harrell, *Security Interests in Deposit Accounts: A Unique Relationship Between the UCC and Other Law*, 23 UCC L.J. 153 (1990). For more detailed discussion of revised Article 9's attachment, perfection, and priority rules governing security interests in deposit accounts and bank setoff rights, *see* WILLIAM H. LAWRENCE ET AL., UNDERSTANDING SECURED TRANSACTIONS §§ 6.04, 10.03 (2d ed. 1999).

(c) *If Lender receives a bill or invoice for an Imposition, Lender shall pay the Imposition from the Imposition Deposits held by Lender. Lender shall have no obligation to pay any Imposition to the extent it exceeds Imposition Deposits then held by Lender. Lender may pay an Imposition according to any bill, statement or estimate from the appropriate public office or insurance company without inquiring into the accuracy of the bill, statement or estimate or into the validity of the Imposition.*

Explanation

What if the lender pays the wrong bill?   Under paragraph 7(c) of the Deed of Trust, the lender is protected in paying any bills from appropriate public offices without inquiring into their accuracy, and agrees that it will pay such bills. The lender is not obligated to pay bills if the escrow account is short. If the lender had to pay such bills, it would be agreeing to make additional loans to the borrower. The lender wants to retain the right to decide if it is in the lender's best interest to make an advance for the benefit of the borrower or to protect the mortgaged property.

(d) If at any time the amount of the Imposition Deposits held by Lender for payment of a specific Imposition exceeds the amount reasonably deemed necessary by Lender, the excess shall be credited against future installments of Imposition Deposits. If at any time the amount of the Imposition Deposits held by Lender for payment of a specific Imposition is less than the amount reasonably estimated by Lender to be necessary, Borrower shall pay to Lender the amount of the deficiency within 15 days after notice from Lender.

Explanation

Does the lender have to return excess escrow funds to the borrower? Under paragraph 7(d), if the lender has collected more escrow funds than needed to pay the escrow items, not only does the lender not have to pay interest as provided in paragraph 7(b), but it does not have to return the monies to the borrower. At the same time, if the lender "reasonably estimates" that the escrow monies will be insufficient to pay escrow items, it can demand that the borrower pay more into escrow within 15 days. If the borrower fails to make the demanded payment, this constitutes a default under paragraph 22(a). The commercial borrower is not protected against overcharging for escrows by this paragraph or by any federal law. In contrast, in the residential loan context, the Real Estate Settlement Procedures Act provides that a lender may not require the borrower to deposit in any escrow account an aggregate sum in excess of a sum that will be sufficient to pay such charges in accordance with a statutory formula. 12 U.S.C. § 2609. Regulation X sets out a very lengthy and complex regulatory protection scheme for the protection of borrowers. 61 Fed. Reg. 10,440 (1996).

(e) If an Event of Default has occurred and is continuing, Lender may apply any Imposition Deposits, in any amounts and in any order as Lender determines, in Lender's discretion, to pay any Impositions or as a credit against the Indebtedness. Upon payment in full of the Indebtedness, Lender shall refund to Borrower any Imposition Deposits held by Lender.

Explanation

The use of escrow money after default.   Paragraph 7(e) provides that if default occurs, the lender can apply escrow monies as the lender determines. The lender will be better off if it does apply the money in reduction of indebtedness prior to the borrower's filing any bankruptcy, in order to avoid any claim by the borrower or trustee that the escrow is "cash collateral." The Bankruptcy Code defines "cash collateral" as "cash, deposit accounts or other cash equivalents in which the estate and an entity other than the assets have an interest and includes the proceeds, products, offspring, rents or profits of property . . . subject to a security interest." 11 U.S.C. § 363(a). The Bankruptcy Code further provides that the bankrupt debtor may not use cash collateral unless: "(A) each entity that has an interest in such cash collateral consents; or (B) the court, after notice and a hearing, authorizes such use." 11 U.S.C. § 363(c)(2). Furthermore, the bankruptcy court may, at any time on request of an entity with an interest in property that the debtor proposes to use, "prohibit or condition such use . . . as is necessary to provide adequate protection of such interest." 11 U.S.C. § 363(e). To the extent that the lender has not applied escrow monies pre-petition, the lender is leaving open to the borrower the potential to obtain a court order authorizing the debtor to use the escrow money.

Collateral Agreements

Borrower shall deposit with Lender such amounts as may be required by any Collateral Agreement and shall perform all other obligations of Borrower under each Collateral Agreement.

Explanation

What is a "collateral agreement"? As defined at paragraph 1(b) of the Deed of Trust, "collateral agreement" encompasses any variety of agreement between the lender and borrower establishing a fund, reserve, or account. Some common types of collateral agreements are replacement reserve agreements, completion-of-repair agreements, and occupancy or income reserve agreements. These agreements may be designed to protect the lender against a specific feature of the collateral or income that is below the lender's desired underwriting standards for the principal amount, interest rate, or credit rating of the borrower or property. For example, a lender may have underwritten a "permanent" loan during construction based on the expectation that the property would be 90 percent leased by the time of the expected closing of the lender's take-out financing. A significant tenant may have not materialized, but the market may indicate that the borrower will likely achieve the desired leasing level in the near term. Rather than fund the loan purely on a reduced amount, a lender may agree to hold back some portion of the

59

loan funds and to fund the held-back amount upon achievement of the leasing. The lender will retain the held-back amount in reserve account.

As another example, a lender may require that the loan-to-value ratio for the loan should not exceed 80 percent. The appraisal may state that the value of the property, if the roof were replaced, would be sufficient. The borrower may be motivated—by reason of a purchase money transaction, a loan commitment expiration, or the running of a 1031 exchange time period—to complete the closing prior to repairing the roof. The lender may be willing to allow the loan to be closed prior to the repair, so long as a sufficient amount of principal is withheld pending completion of the repair to protect its 80 percent loan-to-value criteria.

What if the borrower defaults under a collateral agreement?
Paragraph 8 of the Deed of Trust provides that the borrower will deposit such monies and perform such obligations as may be provided in any collateral agreement. Of course, the collateral agreement itself will require the borrower to fulfill these obligations. The collateral agreement may also specify that a default in the borrower's obligations under the collateral agreement entitles the lender to foreclose under the Deed of Trust. By so providing in the Deed of Trust, paragraph 8 makes it clear of public record that the failure by borrower to pay or perform under a collateral agreement is an event of default under the Deed of Trust.

Application of Payments

If at any time Lender receives, from Borrower or otherwise, any amount applicable to the Indebtedness which is less than all amounts due and payable at such time, then Lender may apply that payment to amounts then due and payable in any manner and in any order determined by Lender, in Lender's discretion. Neither Lender's acceptance of an amount which is less than all amounts then due and payable nor Lender's application of such payment in the manner authorized shall constitute or be deemed to constitute either a waiver of the unpaid amounts or an accord and satisfaction. Notwithstanding the application of any such amount to the Indebtedness, Borrower's obligations under this Instrument and the Note shall remain unchanged.

Explanation

Irregular borrower payments.   The Deed of Trust and the note it secures call for the borrower to make payments to the lender in certain amounts and at certain times. Often, however, borrowers do not pay exactly those amounts at exactly those times. These variances in payment can occur over a period of time—often when a borrower is in financial trouble, or even when a lender may be attempting to assist a borrower. The acceptance by a lender of partial payments or irregular payments can create a course of dealing or waiver against that lender at common law. If a lender accelerates the loan balance due to default and then accepts a monthly payment tendered by the borrower, such acceptance can be deemed to "deaccelerate" or "reinstate" the loan at common law.

Paragraph 9 of the Deed of Trust attempts to protect the lender from such common-law arguments. The borrower agrees that the lender's acceptance of less than the amount due does not constitute a waiver. The borrower agrees that the lender can apply monies in any manner determined by the lender instead of a manner designated by the borrower or as previously applied by the lender.

Accord and satisfaction.   In addition to a waiver or a course of dealing, acceptance by the lender of partial payments under certain circumstances may constitute an accord and satisfaction. An accord and satisfaction is a type of contract whereby one party agrees to give or perform, and the other party agrees to accept, what is offered in settlement of an outstanding claim. In other words, a borrower may claim that she and the lender had entered into a new arrangement whereby the borrower would pay a lesser amount in satisfaction of her obligations. When this contract, or accord, is executed, the underlying claim is deemed satisfied. Pepper's Steel & Alloys, Inc. v. Lissner Materials and Metals, Inc., 494 F. Supp. 487 (S.D.N.Y. 1979). "Until performance of the accord, the original duty is suspended unless there is such a breach of the accord by the obligor as discharges the new duty of the obligee to accept the performance in satisfaction." RESTATEMENT (SECOND) OF CONTRACTS § 281(2). The new accord contract subsumes the original obligation only so long as the accord is not breached. If breach of the accord occurs, the obligee may sue on either the accord or underlying obligation.

Accord and satisfaction must contain all the essentials of a valid contract: competent parties, offer and acceptance, meeting of the minds, and proper consideration. 1 C.J.S. *Accord & Satisfaction* § 10; *see also In re* Koushel, 6 B.R. 315 (Bankr. E.D. Va. 1980); McKibben v. Mohawk Oil Co. Ltd., 667 P.2d 1223 (Alaska 1983). Of critical importance for present purposes is the requirement of consideration. Consideration is deemed to support the promise by an obligee to accept substituted performance where *the existence or amount of the claim is subject to good faith dispute; see* RESTATEMENT (SECOND) OF CONTRACTS § 281 cmt. d. Most states follow the general rule that partial payment of a liquidated and undisputed debt, presently due, "affords no consideration for the discharge of the balance, and so in most jurisdictions cannot affect an accord and satisfaction." 1 C.J.S. *Accord & Satisfaction* § 37(a). (*citing* Roth Steel Tube Co. v. Comm'r of Internal Revenue, 620 F.2d 1176 (6th Cir. 1980); Jefferson Standard Life Ins. Co. v. Lightsey, 49 F.2d 586 (4th Cir.

1931); and case law from 31 states). However, partial payment of a liquidated and undisputed debt may affect an accord and satisfaction if supported by new and separate consideration, however small.[2] 1 C.J.S.
Accord & Satisfaction § 38. Some states have removed the strict requirement of consideration by providing that partial payment by a debtor, expressly accepted in satisfaction, extinguishes the obligation despite
inadequate consideration; *see* 1 C.J.S. *Accord & Satisfaction* § 35 (*citing*
Eberle v. McKeown, 159 N.W.2d 391 (S.D. 1968); Dobinson v.
McDonald, 27 P. 1098 (Cal. 1891); Phinizy v. Bush, 59 S.E. 259 (Ga.
1907); Fuller v. Smith, 77 A. 706 (Me. 1910); and Garland v. Linville
Improvement Co., 115 S.E.164 (N.C. 1922)).

An accord and satisfaction through partial payment will obtain only
where the borrower expressly creates "the condition that the money, if accepted, is to be accepted as, and to constitute full satisfaction, and should be
of such character that the creditor is bound to understand therefrom that, if
he takes the money offered, he takes it subject to such condition." 1 C.J.S.
Accord & Satisfaction § 51 (*citing* Nelson v. Chicago Mill & Lumber Corp.,
76 F.2d 17 (8th Cir. 1935); Pitts v. National Independent Fisheries Co., 206
P. 571 (Colo. 1922); Hanley Co. v. American Cement Co., 143 A. 566
(Conn. 1928); Cole Associates, Inc. v. Holsman, 391 N.E.2d 1196 (Ind.
App. 1979); Shahan v. Bayer Vehicle Co., 162 N.W. 221 (Iowa 1917); Pipes
v. Jesse F. Heard & Sons, Inc., 258 So. 2d 187 (La. App. 1972); Whitcomb
v. Horman, 224 A.2d 120 (Md. App. 1966); Long v. New England
Securities Co., 297 S.W. 715 (Mo. App. 1927); Lovekin v. Fairbanks, Morse
& Co., 127 A. 450 (Pa. 1925); H.L. "Brownie" Choate, Inc. v. Southern
Drilling Co., 447 S.W.2d 676 (Tex. 1969); and Three Rivers Growers' Ass'n
v. Pacific Fruit & Produce Co., 294 P. 233 (Wash. 1930)).

The most common circumstance implicating the law of accord and
satisfaction involves the use by borrowers or consumers of checks
marked "payment in full." Creditors that cash these checks can be held
to have completed an accord and satisfaction, extinguishing their right
to recover the balance due. U.C.C. § 3-311 directly addresses this issue
by limiting the instances where these checks may effect an accord and
satisfaction. Under the U.C.C., a creditor may lose its right to recover

---

[2] Other states provide the exception that where the debtor is known to be "insolvent, or
seriously embarrassed financially," the creditor may accept less than is presently due and effect
an accord and satisfaction of the underlying debt. 1 C.J.S. *Accord & Satisfaction* § 41(a). Also,
where a debtor may lawfully take advantage of the bankruptcy laws—but forbears from doing
so—this forbearance may serve as consideration supporting the promise of the obligee to accept less in satisfaction of the underlying debt. *Id.* § 41(b).

an outstanding balance where the debtor, *in good faith*, tenders the check as full satisfaction of the claim, the amount of the claim is *unliquidated or subject to a bona fide dispute*, and the creditor *obtained payment* of the instrument. U.C.C. § 3-311(a). Thus, the U.C.C. adopts the majority rule that the acceptance of substituted performance by the obligee lacks consideration unless the amount or existence of the debt is subject to a good-faith dispute.

If a creditor has inadvertently accepted a check indicating "full satisfaction," it may return the check to the debtor within 90 days without losing the right to the balance owed. U.C.C. § 3-311(c)(2). In addition, institutional lenders and creditors may establish special offices to handle disputed debts. If the "full satisfaction" check is not sent to the correct office, then debtor may not successfully assert accord and satisfaction. U.C.C. § 3-311(c)(1).

Paragraph 9 of the Deed of Trust firmly establishes that mere acceptance of partial payment without more does not constitute an accord and satisfaction. Partial payment must be accepted under the conditions set forth in U.C.C. § 3-311(a) to put the lender on notice of the conditions attached to acceptance of the money, and to create a valid accord contract. An accord and satisfaction must be accomplished through agreement and supported by adequate consideration where state law requires.

Compliance
with Laws

Borrower shall comply with all laws, ordinances, regulations and requirements of any Governmental Authority and all recorded lawful covenants and agreements relating to or affecting the Mortgaged Property, including all laws, ordinances, regulations, requirements and covenants pertaining to health and safety, construction of improvements on the Mortgaged Property, fair housing, zoning and land use, and Leases. Borrower also shall comply with all applicable laws that pertain to the maintenance and disposition of tenant security deposits. Borrower shall at all times maintain records sufficient to demonstrate compliance with the provisions of this Section 10. Borrower shall take appropriate measures to prevent, and shall not engage in or knowingly permit, any illegal activities at the Mortgaged Property that could endanger tenants or visitors, result in damage to the Mortgaged Property, result in forfeiture of the Mortgaged Property, or otherwise materially impair the lien created by this Instrument or Lender's interest in the Mortgaged Property. Borrower represents and warrants to Lender that no portion of the Mortgaged Property has been or will be purchased with the proceeds of any illegal activity.

Explanation

Why does the lender care if the borrower complies with laws? If a borrower does not comply with laws affecting the property, and the lender forecloses and takes over the property, the lender has a problem.

65

The lender may obtain ownership of a property that requires expensive corrective action to operate or sell. For example, if the borrower builds an improvement or maintains the property in such a way that it comes out of compliance with building codes, the lender may not be able to sell the property without bringing the property into compliance. The zoning authority typically will not issue a certificate of occupancy for the property for the benefit of the buyer without the property being in compliance with building and zoning ordinances. Paragraph 10 attempts to protect the lender against this risk by obligating the borrower to comply with applicable laws and regulations governing the mortgaged property.

Paragraph 10 also attempts to protect the lender against illegal activities occurring on the property. If the borrower engages in or does not prevent illegal activities, this would be an event of default under paragraph 22 of the Deed of Trust.

Forfeiture.   If a borrower engages in or does not prevent illegal activities, the mortgaged property may be subject to forfeiture under various state and federal statutes. Such statutes typically provide an "innocent owner" defense that protects the lender's security interest in the property. For example, the Comprehensive Crime Control Act of 1984, 21 U.S.C. § 881(a)(7), provides that "no property shall be forfeited . . . to the extent of an interest of an owner, by reason of any act or omission established by that owner to have been committed or omitted without the knowledge or consent of that owner." The Uniform Controlled Substances Act, adopted in whole or in part by every state, provides that

> an interest in property acquired by an owner before the occurrence of conduct that subjects the property to forfeiture is exempt from forfeiture if: (1) the owner did not know the conduct would occur at the time of acquisition of the interest and at any later time when an actor controlled or possessed the property; or (2) the owner acted in a manner the owner reasonably believed appropriate to prevent an actor's conduct and assist in the prosecution of the actor [§ 505(b) (1994)].

Some state civil forfeiture statutes do not provide an innocent owner defense, and this has been held to not violate the innocent owner's constitutional rights. Bennis v. Michigan, 116 S.Ct. 994 (1996).

In a typical forfeiture proceeding, the government must first establish probable cause that the claimant's property was used in violation of some criminal statute providing for forfeiture of property. If probable cause is shown, the burden shifts to the claimant to prove the innocent owner defense. First, the claimant must demonstrate standing to file a claim to the property. Standing may be established through showing that the claimant has an ownership interest in the property. In *United States v. Federal Nat'l Mortgage Ass'n*, 946 F.2d 264 (4th Cir. 1991), the court held that a lien holder is an "owner" for purposes of 21 U.S.C. § 881. The Uniform Controlled Substances Act defines an "owner" as "a person who has a legal or equitable interest in property, including a security interest." (§ 501 (1994)).

Pursuant to 21 U.S.C. § 881, to avoid forfeiture, the claimant must prove that the underlying criminal activities were committed or omitted without the claimant's knowledge or consent. The court in *United States v. 6960 Miraflores Ave.*, 995 F.2d 1558 (11th Cir. 1993), held that the claimant must demonstrate his lack of *actual* knowledge of the crime in order to prevail in its innocent owner defense. If the claimant obtains its interest in the property after the illegal act has occurred, the court must examine the issue of claimant's knowledge at the time of the property transfer. United States v. 6640 S.W. 48th St., 831 F. Supp. 1578 (S.D. Fla. 1993).

The circuits remain divided over whether the phrase "without the knowledge or consent" must be read in the conjunctive or the disjunctive. The Ninth Circuit has taken the position that the claimant is required to demonstrate both lack of knowledge and lack of consent. United States v. Lot 111-B, 902 F.2d 1143 (9th Cir. 1990). The Second, Third, and Eleventh Circuits, however, have held that the claimant is required to demonstrate only a lack of knowledge or lack of consent. According to this view, a property owner who has actual knowledge of drug activity can still avoid forfeiture by establishing that the offense took place without his consent. United States v. 141st St. Corp., 911 F.2d 870 (2nd Cir. 1990); United States v. 6109 Grubb Rd., 886 F.2d 618 (3d Cir. 1989); United States v. 1012 Germantown Rd., 963 F.2d 1496 (11th Cir. 1992). Under the Uniform Controlled Substances Act, if the owner has knowledge of the illegal activity, it must demonstrate that it acted in a manner the owner reasonably believed appropriate to prevent the illegal conduct and must assist in the prosecution of the actor.

If the lien holder is successful in establishing the innocent owner defense, the forfeiture to the government is subject to the claimant's claims for principal, preseizure and postseizure interest, and, if provided for in the mortgage documents, the lien holder's costs and lawyer's fees incurred in obtaining its interests. United States v. Federal Nat'l Mortgage Ass'n, 946 F.2d 264 (4th Cir. 1991).

Use of Property

Unless required by applicable law, Borrower shall not (a) except for any change in use approved by Lender, allow changes in the use for which all or any part of the Mortgaged Property is being used at the time this Instrument was executed, (b) convert any individual dwelling units or common areas to commercial use, (c) initiate or acquiesce in a change in the zoning classification of the Mortgaged Property, or (d) establish any condominium or cooperative regime with respect to the Mortgaged Property.

Explanation

Restrictions on changes in use.   A mortgage lender wants to make certain that it can maintain control over and prevent any changes in the property, or its use, that might devalue the property as security for the mortgage loan. Under this Deed of Trust, the lender would be making a mortgage loan against the security of a multifamily residential project; paragraph 11 of the Deed of Trust thus protects the lender against certain obvious use changes that would fundamentally alter the project in a manner inconsistent with its operation as a multi-family apartment building. In mortgages on other types of commercial property, even more extensive limitations and lender approval requirements may be imposed.

Protection of Lender's Security

(a) If Borrower fails to perform any of its obligations under this Instrument or any other Loan Document, or if any action or proceeding is commenced which purports to affect the Mortgaged Property, Lender's security or Lender's rights under this Instrument, including eminent domain, insolvency, code enforcement, civil or criminal forfeiture, enforcement of Hazardous Materials Laws, fraudulent conveyance or reorganizations or proceedings involving a bankrupt or decedent, then Lender at Lender's option may make such appearances, disburse such sums and take such actions as Lender reasonably deems necessary to perform such obligations of Borrower and to protect Lender's interest, including (1) payment of fees and out-of-pocket expenses of attorneys, accountants, inspectors and consultants, (2) entry upon the Mortgaged Property to make repairs or secure the Mortgaged Property, (3) procurement of the insurance required by Section 19, and (4) payment of amounts which Borrower has failed to pay under Sections 15 and 17.

Explanation

Does self-help work for the lender? Paragraph 12(a) amounts to a "self-help" paragraph for the benefit of the lender. This self-help concept is applicable in some circumstances and not others and is more effective in some circumstances than in others. For example, this paragraph allows

71

the lender to take actions that it deems necessary in the event of the institution of an eminent domain proceeding that affects the property. Because a mortgage lender has an interest in the property, the lender is likely a necessary party defendant in eminent domain proceedings in any event. A mortgage lender, in the absence of some contractual provision to the contrary, will be entitled in those proceedings to receive the value of the estate subject to its lien up to the dollar amount of its lien. Paragraph 12(a) adds nothing and takes nothing away from the lender's position in this regard. Insolvency is another example of a situation in which the self-help concept appears irrelevant. If the borrower files a bankruptcy petition, the lender may appear in the proceedings and assert its secured claim whether this paragraph were in the Deed of Trust or not.

In contrast, the self-help remedy in paragraph 12(a) is a valuable tool in instances of code violations or failure of the borrower to maintain the property, to maintain insurance, or to pay taxes. These are all borrower failures that the lender can meaningfully step in and perform. If the lender corrects these failures by the borrower, it helps its collateral position by helping to preserve the value of its collateral.

Paragraph 12(a) also helps the lender by specifying that to the extent the lender incurs expenses of attorneys, accountants, inspectors, or consultants in any of these instances, it can recover those amounts from the borrower. Some states have statutory provisions that allow lenders to add such items to the debt regardless of whether the loan documents so provide. For example, a Missouri statute permits recovery of lawyers' fees expended to enforce a credit agreement, even if not provided for in the credit agreement, if: (1) the enforcing lawyer is a licensed member of the Missouri bar or is authorized to practice law in Missouri, (2) the fees do not exceed 15 percent of the outstanding credit balance in default, and (3) the credit was extended by a for-profit business or credit union. R.S. Mo. § 408.092.

(b) *Any amounts disbursed by Lender under this Section 12, or under any other provision of this Instrument that treats such disbursement as being made under this Section 12, shall be added to, and become part of, the principal component of the Indebtedness, shall be immediately due and payable and shall bear interest from the date of disbursement until paid at the "Default Rate" as defined in the Note.*

Explanation

Is it fair for the lender to earn a premium interest rate on advances?

The borrower agrees in the Deed of Trust to maintain the property, obtain insurance, pay taxes, and perform other obligations. If the borrower does not live up to those obligations, the lender can expend the sums needed to do so. If the lender has to advance more of its own money to do so, the lender is specifying that it is going to earn a premium interest rate for its inconvenience. The lender can also justify this result because it is having to advance additional sums in the face of a default by borrower—which means that the lender is making a more risky loan, for which lenders typically charge a higher rate of interest.

(c) *Nothing in this Section 12 shall require Lender to incur any expense or take any action.*

Explanation

Does the lender have to maintain the mortgaged property? The lender does not want the borrower to be under any misunderstanding or impression; the fact that the mortgage authorizes the lender to take such actions and spend such monies as are needed to fulfill the borrower's maintenance and performance obligations *does not* mean that the lender is obligated to do so or even that the lender will do so. As paragraph 12(c) of the Deed of Trust provides, the lender's performance of such actions is optional and should be in the lender's sole discretion. The lender may decide that expending any sums in a particular circumstance amounts to "throwing good money after bad." The lender may have no hope of recovery of its investment. The lender may conclude on its own that spending the additional monies will not increase the recovery by the lender and may only serve to increase the equity available to the borrower.

Inspection

Lender, its agents, representatives, and designees may make or cause to be made entries upon and inspections of the Mortgaged Property (including environmental inspections and tests) during normal business hours, or at any other reasonable time.

Explanation

Who says what you don't know won't hurt you?   Paragraph 13 of the Deed of Trust authorizes the lender to inspect the property. Lenders underwrite mortgage loans on the basis of varying criteria—but one of these will nearly always be the value of the property as collateral. Value is a function of many factors, but the physical condition and state of repair of the property are always relevant. If a mortgage lender has initially underwritten the loan based on the property having a certain value and being in a certain physical condition, the lender wants the right to inspect the property at the lender's convenience to confirm that the value remains consistent with the lender's underwriting assumptions.

Books and Records; Financial Reporting

(a) Borrower shall keep and maintain at all times at the Mortgaged Property or the management agent's offices, and upon Lender's request shall make available at the Mortgaged Property, complete and accurate books of account and records (including copies of supporting bills and invoices) adequate to reflect correctly the operation of the Mortgaged Property, and copies of all written contracts, Leases, and other instruments which affect the Mortgaged Property. The books, records, contracts, Leases and other instruments shall be subject to examination and inspection at any reasonable time by Lender.

(b) Borrower shall furnish to Lender all of the following:

   (1) within 120 days after the end of each fiscal year of Borrower, a statement of income and expenses for Borrower's operation of the Mortgaged Property for that fiscal year, a statement of changes in financial position of Borrower relating to the Mortgaged Property for that fiscal year and, when requested by Lender, a balance sheet showing all assets and liabilities of Borrower relating to the Mortgaged Property as of the end of that fiscal year;

   (2) within 120 days after the end of each fiscal year of Borrower, and at any other time upon Lender's request, a rent schedule for the Mortgaged Property showing the name of each tenant, and for each tenant, the space occupied, the lease expiration date, the rent

77

payable for the current month, the date through which rent has been paid, and any related information requested by Lender;

(3) *within 120 days after the end of each fiscal year of Borrower, and at any other time upon Lender's request, an accounting of all security deposits held pursuant to all Leases, including the name of the institution (if any) and the names and identification numbers of the accounts (if any) in which such security deposits are held and the name of the person to contact at such financial institution, along with any authority or release necessary for Lender to access information regarding such accounts;*

(4) *within 120 days after the end of each fiscal year of Borrower, and at any other time upon Lender's request, a statement that identifies all owners of any interest in Borrower and the interest held by each, if Borrower is a corporation, all officers and directors of Borrower, and if Borrower is a limited liability company, all managers who are not members;*

(5) *upon Lender's request, a monthly property management report for the Mortgaged Property, showing the number of inquiries made and rental applications received from tenants or prospective tenants and deposits received from tenants and any other information requested by Lender;*

(6) *upon Lender's request, a balance sheet, a statement of income and expenses for Borrower and a statement of changes in financial position of Borrower for Borrower's most recent fiscal year; and*

(7) *if required by Lender, a statement of income and expense for the Mortgaged Property for the prior month or quarter.*

(c) *Each of the statements, schedules and reports required by Section 14(b) shall be certified to be complete and accurate by an individual having authority to bind Borrower, and shall be in such form and contain such detail as Lender may reasonably require. Lender also may require that any statements, schedules or reports be audited at Borrower's expense by independent certified public accountants acceptable to Lender.*

(d) *If Borrower fails to provide in a timely manner the statements, schedules and reports required by Section 14(b), Lender shall have the right to have Borrower's books and records audited, at Borrower's expense, by independent certified public accountants selected by Lender in order to obtain such statements, schedules and reports, and all related costs and expenses of Lender shall become immediately due and payable and shall become an additional part of the Indebtedness as provided in Section 12.*

(e) If an Event of Default has occurred and is continuing, Borrower shall deliver to Lender upon written demand all books and records relating to the Mortgaged Property or its operation.

(f) Borrower authorizes Lender to obtain a credit report on Borrower at any time.

(g) If an Event of Default has occurred and Lender has not previously required Borrower to furnish a quarterly statement of income and expense for the Mortgaged Property, Lender may require Borrower to furnish such a statement within 45 days after the end of each fiscal quarter of Borrower following such Event of Default.

Explanation

Monitoring the loan and the mortgaged property.   Another criterion lenders use to underwrite loans on commercial property is the income-producing ability of the property. If the loan will require payments of $10,000 per month to remain current, the lender will require that the property generate income in excess of that amount so that the property can support the loan payments together with the expenses of operating and maintaining the property. Paragraph 14(a) of the Deed of Trust requires the borrower to maintain accurate books of account and authorizes the lender to inspect those records.

Paragraph 14(b) goes beyond the inspection rights granted to the lender in paragraph 14(a), requiring the borrower to provide the lender with a series of annual and monthly financial reports. Paragraph 14(b) also allows the lender to request certain reports whenever it chooses. The reports included in paragraph 14(b) allow the lender to monitor the financial health of the property and include income and expense statements, balance sheets, rent schedules, an accounting of security deposits held, and financial statements of those holding equity interests in the borrower.

Certified financial reports.   Paragraph 14(c) requires that all of the financial statements "be certified to be complete and accurate by an individual having authority to bind Borrower." This certification is designed to create liability if the statements turn out not to be true. Paragraph 14(c) also allows the lender to require that any statement be audited at the borrower's expense. This is a potentially expensive right the lender is allowing itself.

The lender's right to audit the borrower.   Under paragraph 14(d), if the borrower "fails to provide in a timely manner the statements," then the lender has the right to have the borrower's books and records audited. To a large degree, the value of commercial real estate is not the real estate itself but the income the real estate is able to generate. A failure on the part of the borrower to provide a requested financial report should set off a warning bell. The Deed of Trust gives the lender the right to protect itself against the threats signaled by that warning bell. Nevertheless, paragraph 14(d) is unrealistic: If the borrower is refusing to turn over reports for a reason, the borrower is unlikely to open its door to the auditor in a cooperative manner.

Paragraph 14(e) is also unrealistic. What borrower is going to default on a loan and then go to the time, trouble, and effort to deliver its books and records to the lender? Both paragraphs 14(d) and 14(e) are really designed to enhance the lender's position in litigation. Their inclusion in the Deed of Trust may be a sufficient basis to enable the lender to obtain a receivership order that includes an audit right and delivery of books and records.

Paragraph 14(f) is designed to protect the lender from liability for obtaining unauthorized credit reports. Paragraph 14(g) adds very little benefit, given that paragraph 14(b)(7) already allows the lender to require quarterly income and expense statements for any reason.

Taxes; Operating Expenses

(a) Subject to the provisions of Section 15(c) and Section 15(d), Borrower shall pay, or cause to be paid, all Taxes when due and before the addition of any interest, fine, penalty or cost for nonpayment.

(b) Subject to the provisions of Section 15(c), Borrower shall pay the expenses of operating, managing, maintaining and repairing the Mortgaged Property (including insurance premiums, utilities, repairs and replacements) before the last date upon which each such payment may be made without any penalty or interest charge being added.

(c) As long as no Event of Default exists and Borrower has timely delivered to Lender any bills or premium notices that it has received, Borrower shall not be obligated to pay Taxes, insurance premiums or any other individual Imposition to the extent that sufficient Imposition Deposits are held by Lender for the purpose of paying that specific Imposition. If an Event of Default exists, Lender may exercise any rights Lender may have with respect to Imposition Deposits without regard to whether Impositions are then due and payable. Lender shall have no liability to Borrower for failing to pay any Impositions to the extent that any Event of Default has occurred and is continuing, insufficient Imposition Deposits are held by Lender at the time an Imposition becomes due and payable or Borrower has failed to provide Lender with bills and premium notices as provided above.

(d) Borrower, at its own expense, may contest by appropriate legal proceedings, conducted diligently and in good faith, the amount or validity

> *of any Imposition other than insurance premiums, if (1) Borrower no-*
> *tifies Lender of the commencement or expected commencement of such*
> *proceedings, (2) the Mortgaged Property is not in danger of being sold*
> *or forfeited, (3) Borrower deposits with Lender reserves sufficient to pay*
> *the contested Imposition, if requested by Lender, and (4) Borrower fur-*
> *nishes whatever additional security is required in the proceedings or is*
> *reasonably requested by Lender, which may include the delivery to*
> *Lender of the reserves established by Borrower to pay the contested*
> *Imposition.*
>
> *(e) Borrower shall promptly deliver to Lender a copy of all notices of, and in-*
> *voices for, Impositions, and if Borrower pays any Imposition directly,*
> *Borrower shall promptly furnish to Lender receipts evidencing such pay-*
> *ments.*

Explanation

Payment of taxes.   Paragraph 15(a) of the Deed of Trust is an affirmative covenant on the borrower's part to pay all "taxes." Paragraph 1(y)
of the Deed of Trust defines the term "taxes" very broadly to include
governmental and quasi-governmental impositions against the land and
improvements constituting the security for the loan that, if not paid,
would become a lien. It is important for a lender to make sure that the
borrower has paid all of the taxes affecting the security prior to delinquency, because delinquent taxes will typically afford the taxing authority a "priming" lien on the real property—i.e., a lien that is superior
to any security interest of the lender. By adding a specific covenant to
the Deed of Trust requiring the borrower to pay the taxes, the lender affords itself a right to cure the borrower's failure to pay such taxes under
the default provisions of the Deed of Trust and to add the costs of cure
to the amounts secured by the Deed of Trust.

**Payment of expenses of operating, maintaining, and repairing the
mortgaged property.**   Paragraph 15(b) is an affirmative covenant on
the borrower's part to pay all costs associated with operating and maintaining the property. A well-maintained and well-operated property is
more valuable to a lender for several reasons. Most obviously, the lender
wishes to avoid waste and deterioration of the real property and improvements securing the loan. Just as important, however, is the ability
to attract and retain tenants on the property. Typically, the cash flow
necessary to maintain debt service is obtained through the payment of
rent pursuant to leases on the property. If the property is not properly

managed and maintained, it will be difficult to attract and retain tenants, and this may jeopardize the ability of the borrower to repay the loan. Failure to maintain the real property may also provide tenants with an opportunity to terminate their leases and/or expose the landlord (and a lender succeeding to the interest of the landlord through foreclosure) to potential liability, if tenants have the right to cure a failure to maintain the property and seek reimbursement. In addition, if another party makes repairs on the property and fails to make payment for those repairs, this failure may (depending upon the jurisdiction) provide the repairing party with a lien for the costs of such repairs, and this lien may be superior to the lender's mortgage.

Similar to the treatment of taxes in paragraph 15(a), paragraph 15(b) provides the lender with an opportunity to declare a default if the costs of operating and maintaining the property are not paid, and to cure such default. The lender will typically give itself the right to add the costs of cure to the amount secured by the Deed of Trust. *See supra* Section 12.

Imposition deposits. Paragraph 15(c) clarifies many of the lender's rights and obligations with respect to the imposition deposits addressed in paragraph 7 of the Deed of Trust. First, paragraph 15(c) relieves the borrower of the responsibility to pay taxes and impositions to the extent the lender has received escrows for such impositions, the borrower has provided the lender with notices of the amounts to be paid, and the borrower is not in default. Paragraph 15(e) places an affirmative obligation upon the borrower to provide the lender with notice of the amount and due date of such impositions. As discussed in Section 7, the lender is obligated to apply the imposition deposits to the expenses for which the lender is escrowing. However, paragraph 15(c) limits the lender's liability for failure to perform its obligation to the extent the borrower has committed an event of default or has failed to provide the lender with bills and premium notices. In addition, paragraph 15(c) permits the lender to apply the imposition deposits to the borrower's debt in the event of a default, if permitted under the laws of the applicable jurisdiction. If the lender exercises that right, it will not be responsible for paying the impositions to the extent it has depleted the imposition deposits by applying the deposits to the indebtedness.

Contests. A borrower will generally want the right to contest any impositions in the event the borrower believes that the government or other party has improperly levied or applied that imposition against the property. Lenders will typically permit borrowers the opportunity to contest such impositions, provided the lender is comfortable that its security will not be impaired. Paragraph 15(d) of the Deed of Trust permits the borrower to contest impositions (other than insurance premiums, which are a matter of contract between the borrower and insurer), provided that the borrower notifies the lender of the contest, the property is not in jeopardy of being lost, and the borrower provides the lender with security against a determination that the imposition was properly assessed. With such notice and security, the lender can monitor the contest to ensure that its security is not impaired. In the event the contest is determined adversely to the borrower, the borrower may be liable for interest and penalties. The lender will want to make sure that the amount of security received from the borrower is sufficient to cover any such amounts. Among the types of security routinely accepted by lenders are cash deposits, bonds, and letters of credit.

Liens;
Encumbrances

Borrower acknowledges that, to the extent provided in Section 21, the grant, creation or existence of any mortgage, deed of trust, deed to secure debt, security interest or other lien or encumbrance (a "Lien") on the Mortgaged Property (other than the lien of this Instrument) or on certain ownership interests in Borrower, whether voluntary, involuntary or by operation of law, and whether or not such Lien has priority over the lien of this Instrument, is a "Transfer" which constitutes an Event of Default.

Explanation

Why does the lender care about additional liens? Paragraph 16 of the Deed of Trust makes it an event of default for the borrower to permit any lien to attach to the mortgaged property. The lender may then exercise its remedies for the default, including the right to accelerate the indebtedness under paragraph 43. The lender's rationale for this paragraph is that any indebtedness secured by a lien on the mortgaged property, whether prior to or subordinate to the lien of the Deed of Trust, may impair the borrower's ability to pay its debt to the lender. Another underwriting criterion commonly relied upon by commercial lenders is the property's debt service coverage ratio, or DSCR. The DSCR is the ratio of the net expected income generated by the property (after deduction for vacancies and operating expenses) to the dollar amount of payments

85

necessary to service the debt borne by the property. Lenders want to be sure that the DSCR will exceed 1.0, and may require that it be as high as 1.2 or 1.3. In addition, it may be that the priority of some types of liens will not be readily apparent at the time of attachment to the mortgaged property. For example, some mechanics and materialmen's liens may gain priority to the extent of the improvement constructed. Also, a lender will wish to avoid the situation where a lien may gain priority over its mortgage, as (for example) in the event of a modification of the mortgage. Practically, then, the lender may use paragraph 16 in order to afford itself a right of approval with respect to subsequent encumbrances.

Preservation, Management and Maintenance of Mortgaged Property

(a) Borrower (1) shall not commit waste or permit impairment or deterioration of the Mortgaged Property, (2) shall not abandon the Mortgaged Property, (3) shall restore or repair promptly, in a good and workmanlike manner, any damaged part of the Mortgaged Property to the equivalent of its original condition, or such other condition as Lender may approve in writing, whether or not insurance proceeds or condemnation awards are available to cover any costs of such restoration or repair, (4) shall keep the Mortgaged Property in good repair, including the replacement of Personalty and Fixtures with items of equal or better function and quality, (5) shall provide for professional management of the Mortgaged Property by a residential rental property manager satisfactory to Lender under a contract approved by Lender in writing, and (6) shall give notice to Lender of and, unless otherwise directed in writing by Lender, shall appear in and defend any action or proceeding purporting to affect the Mortgaged Property, Lender's security or Lender's rights under this Instrument. Borrower shall not (and shall not permit any tenant or other person to) remove, demolish or alter the Mortgaged Property or any part of the Mortgaged Property except in connection with the replacement of tangible Personalty.

(b) If, in connection with the making of the loan evidenced by the Note or at any later date, Lender waives in writing the requirement of Section 17(a)(5) above that Borrower enter into a written contract for management *of the Mortgaged Property and if, after the date of this Instrument, Borrower intends to change the management of the Mortgaged Property, Lender shall have the right to approve such new property manager and the written contract for the management of the Mortgaged Property and require that Borrower and such new property manager enter into an Assignment of Management Agreement on a form approved by Lender. If required by Lender (whether before or after an Event of Default), Borrower will cause any Affiliate of Borrower to whom fees are payable for the management of the Mortgaged Property to enter into an agreement with Lender, in a form approved by Lender, providing for subordination of those fees and such other provisions as Lender may require. "Affiliate of Borrower" means any corporation, partnership, joint venture, limited liability company, limited liability partnership, trust or individual controlled by, under common control with, or which controls Borrower (the term "control" for these purposes shall mean the ability, whether by the ownership of shares or other equity interests, by contract or otherwise, to elect a majority of the directors of a corporation, to make management decisions on behalf of, or independently to select the managing partner of, a partnership, or otherwise to have the power independently to remove and then select a majority of those individuals exercising managerial authority over an entity, and control shall be conclusively presumed in the case of the ownership of 50% or more of the equity interests).*

Explanation

Waste and management.   The common-law doctrine of waste protects all mortgage lenders, at a minimum making it wrongful for the borrower to damage the security property. The concept of waste has been broadened in recent years, as reflected in Restatement (Third) of Property: Mortgages § 4.6 (1997). Under the Restatement, waste includes not only physical damage to the property, but also failure to repair and maintain it, failure to pay property taxes and assessments, and failure to comply with covenants in the mortgage respecting "physical care, maintenance, construction, demolition, or insurance against casualty." To these requirements, paragraph 17 of the Deed of Trust adds duties of repair or replacement of personal property, the use of a professional property manager, and the defense of any suit affecting the mortgaged property.

Rental property developers often form subsidiary or related corporations to perform property management on their projects. Indeed, management fees provide an important mechanism for the developer to take funds out of the project. Paragraph 17 permits the lender to insist that fees to a developer-related management company be subordinated to all payments due under the loan. One should note that this right in paragraph 17 is *not dependent on the existence of a default*. The subordination mentioned here is not a subordination of a lien, because the management company typically has no lien on the property. Rather, it is a "debt subordination," and allows the lender to prevent any payment from being made to the management company unless all payments under the loan documents are current. *See* Patrick Mears, *Who's on First? Negotiating Debt and Lien Subordination Agreements in Real Estate Transactions*, PROB. & PROP., Jan/Feb. 1999, at 19.

Environmental Hazards

Fannie Mae Form Deed of Trust Environmental Definitions

Definitions.

The following terms, when used in this Instrument (including when used in the above recitals), shall have the following meanings: . . .

c. **"Environmental Permit"** means any permit, license, or other authorization issued under any Hazardous Materials Law with respect to any activities or businesses conducted on or in relation to the Mortgaged Property. . . .

f. **"Governmental Authority"** means any board, commission, department or body of any municipal, county, state or federal governmental unit, or any subdivision of any of them, that has or acquires jurisdiction over the Mortgaged Property or the use, operation or improvement of the Mortgaged Property.

g. **"Hazardous Materials"** means petroleum and petroleum products and compounds containing them, including gasoline, diesel fuel and oil; explosives; flammable materials; radioactive materials; polychlorinated biphenyls ("PCBs") and compounds containing them; lead and lead-based paint; asbestos or asbestos-containing materials in any form that is or could become friable; underground or above-ground storage tanks, whether empty or containing any substance; any substance the presence of which on the Mortgaged Property is prohibited by any federal, state or local authority; any substance that requires special handling; and any other material or substance now or in the future defined as a "hazardous substance," "hazardous material," "hazardous waste," "toxic substance," "toxic pollutant," "contaminant," or "pollutant" within the meaning of any Hazardous Materials Law.

h. **"Hazardous Materials Laws"** means all federal, state, and local laws, ordinances and regulations and standards, rules, policies and other governmental requirements, administrative rulings and court judgments and decrees in effect now or in the future and including all amendments, that relate to Hazardous Materials and apply to Borrower or to the Mortgaged Property. Hazardous Materials Laws include, but are not limited to, the Comprehensive Environmental Response, Compensation and Liability Act, 42 U.S.C. Section 9601, et seq., the Resource Conservation and Recovery Act, 42 U.S.C. Section 6901, et seq., the Toxic Substance Control Act, 15 U.S.C. Section 2601, et seq., the Clean Water Act, 33 U.S.C. Section 1251, et seq., and the Hazardous Materials Transportation Act, 49 U.S.C. Section 5101, et seq., and their state analogs.

Explanation

The beginning point for the discussion of the environmental provisions of paragraph 18 of the Deed of Trust is the definition of "hazardous materials laws." Since 1970, Congress has enacted a flood of environmental statutes, including those listed specifically in the definition contained in paragraph 1. These statutes sweep broadly, making thousands of substances—as well as the businesses, individuals, and others who handle or emit them—subject to extensive and burdensome regulation. For the most part, each of these federal statutes uses the same regulatory approach: A national permit program sets and imposes minimum national standards, preempting less restrictive state regulations. Each state is called upon to enact conforming state laws and regulations and to seek the approval of the U.S. Environmental Protection Agency (EPA) to administer the national program within its borders.

Upon approval, the state becomes the primary permit-issuing and enforcement authority, subject to EPA's power to veto permits and take independent enforcement actions against violators. Where a state chooses not to adopt and run a conforming program, the EPA administers and enforces the permit program in that state.

"Hazardous materials laws." The Comprehensive Environmental Response, Compensation and Liability Act, 42 U.S.C. § 9601 et seq., ("Superfund" or CERCLA) was enacted in 1980 and substantially amended and reenacted in 1986. CERCLA differs from the other federal statutes discussed herein because it has no separate permit program. CERCLA is a comprehensive federal statute that grants the federal government broad powers to force private parties to clean up hazardous waste sites. In addition, CERCLA requires parties to report and clean up any "release" of hazardous substances in excess of the applicable "reportable quantity" as soon as the release occurs. Federal regulations list thousands of hazardous substances and their reportable quantities. The only exception to this reporting duty is a "federally permitted release," which generally covers any discharge or emission made in compliance with a federal or state permit. If, however, the permit holder discharges or emits amounts of a regulated "hazardous substance" into the environment in excess of applicable permit conditions, he must report that violation to the National Response Center, in addition to reporting it to the permitting agency.

CERCLA is the initial focus of environmental provisions because of its draconian liability scheme, which makes CERCLA the most important environmental consideration in real estate lending transactions. Liability under CERCLA is strict; fault and negligence are irrelevant. Liability is retroactive: a party may be held liable for past activities—even those prior to CERCLA's enactment in 1980—that were legal at the time they occurred. The fact that a party complied with all laws and regulations and exercised all due care with regard to the substances does not protect it from liability. Liability is generally joint and several. A defendant bears the burden of showing that the harm is divisible. The commingling of wastes from different potentially responsible parties (PRPs) generally renders the harm indivisible. At sites where several or many parties may have disposed of wastes, proof of divisibility is nearly impossible. Allocation of costs occurs in the secondary proceeding for contribution among the jointly and severally liable parties. Finally, CERCLA's standard of causation is minimal. The issue of causation is reduced to whether a release or threat of release has caused the EPA or a private party to incur response costs. Plaintiff must, however, establish a causal link between the release and the response.

CERCLA imposes liability for the costs of cleanup of a contaminated site or facility on four categories of PRPs: (a) the owners or operators of the site at the time the wastes were deposited; (b) the present owners or operators of such a site; (c) the transporters who delivered hazardous substances to the site; and (d) the persons who arranged for disposal, treatment, or transport of wastes to the site (usually called "generators"). The last category includes businesses that generate and send wastes to off-site disposal locations.

Particularly relevant to a discussion of this section of the Deed of Trust are two "safe harbors" from CERCLA liability: (a) the "secured party" exemption for lenders; and (b) the "innocent purchaser" exemption.

Lender liability.   From the beginning, CERCLA has included an exemption for any secured party that acted "primarily to protect its security interest." Nevertheless, courts have imposed liability on lenders who became "owners" by foreclosing on a deed of trust and buying in the contaminated property at the foreclosure sale (*see, e.g.,* United States v. Maryland Bank & Trust Co., 632 F. Supp. 573 (D. Md. 1986)), or "operators" by participating in the day-to-day operational aspects of the business's hazardous waste activities. (*see, e.g.,* United States v. Mirabile, 23 Env't Rep. Cas. 1511 (E.D. Pa. 1985)). Under this line of authority, once a lender bank became an owner through foreclosure, participated in management through control over its borrower, or became "involve[d] with the management of the facility [in a manner] sufficiently broad to support the inference that it could affect hazardous waste disposal decisions if it so chose" (United States v. Fleet Factors Corp., 31 Env't Rep. Cas. 1465 (11th Cir. 1990)), the bank was no longer exempt from liability as a creditor and thus was liable for cleanup costs.

These developments changed the perspective of lenders dramatically. Before these judicial developments, a lender's risk analysis took into account the possibility that the mortgaged property might be or become contaminated, and that the borrower might not be able to repay the loan. Under these cases, a lender faced the prospect of having to lay out large sums of money to clean up the contamination on the mortgaged property, and thereafter own or have a security interest in a formerly contaminated—and therefore stigmatized and less valuable—parcel of property. The lending community stopped making loans on environmentally risky properties and went to work to address this liability problem.

Following the *Fleet Factors* decision, the courts and Congress revisited the issue of lender liability under CERCLA. For example, the Fourth Circuit found that a lender qualified for CERCLA's secured party exemption from liability even though it had bought a contaminated property at foreclosure. U.S. v. McLamb, 5 F. 3d 69 (4th Cir. 1993). The court said,

> In the instant case, due to the lack of other potential buyers at the foreclosure sale, the lender purchased the property, in the language of the statute, "primarily to protect its security interest" after the default. The record reveals no investment or profit motive for acquiring the property. The lender did not, for example, engage in a bidding war at the foreclosure sale. Further, the lender almost immediately placed the property on the market, took no steps to use or manage the land during its ownership, and ultimately sold the property to the first able buyer. Such steps support its claim that it held title primarily, indeed exclusively, to protect its security interest. [5 F.3d at 72]

The Fourth Circuit in *McLamb* contrasted the lender's actions to those of Maryland Bank & Trust, discussed in *U.S. v. Maryland Bank & Trust, supra.* The loan on which MB&T foreclosed was made in 1980, but MB&T had made earlier loans for 15 years on the property and knew it was used for trash disposal. The foreclosure commenced in 1981, and MB&T bought the property at the foreclosure sale in May 1982. The EPA determined that a cleanup action was warranted, and in 1983 offered MB&T the opportunity to clean it up. After the bank declined, the EPA cleaned up the site and sued the bank for recovery of its costs. The Fourth Circuit remarked that the exemption does not apply "when, as here, the former mortgagee has held title for nearly four years, and a full year before the EPA cleanup." *McLamb*, 5 F.3d at 72 n.6.

The Fourth Circuit also held that the lender in *McLamb* had fulfilled the second prong of the test: no management of the property. "Wachovia did not attempt to develop or manage the property but continued to hold it solely to protect its security interest." *Id.* at 73.

In 1996, Congress enacted the Asset Conservation, Lender Liability, and Deposit Insurance Protection Act. The purpose of the legislation was to clarify lender liability issues under CERCLA. The act amends CERCLA and creates safe harbors for lenders, trustees, and fiduciaries. Lenders who do not exercise decision-making control over contaminated property during the term of a loan or who foreclose on contaminated property and make reasonable attempts to sell the property to protect their security interest are not subject to CERCLA liability as owners.

Innocent purchaser exemption. The owner of property contaminated before it was purchased may be excused from liability if it can show that it had no reason to know of the contamination before the purchase. To make this showing, the landowner must have "undertaken, at the time of acquisition, all appropriate inquiry into the previous ownership and uses of the property consistent with good commercial or customary practice in an effort to minimize liability." *See* CERCLA § 101(35)(A), 42 U.S.C. § 9601(35)(A). The standard is not absolute for all land purchasers: The greater the sophistication of the land purchaser, or the more obvious the contamination, the more difficulty one will have qualifying for this exception from liability. *See, e.g.,* New York v. Lashins, 91 F.3d 353 (2d Cir. 1996) (landowner held to have exercised "due care"). A standard practice has emerged for conducting environmental due diligence assessments to qualify for this exemption. *See* ASTM E1527, STANDARD PRACTICE FOR ENVIRONMENTAL SITE ASSESSMENTS: PHASE I ENVIRONMENTAL SITE ASSESSMENT PROCESS (American Society for Testing and Materials, 1996). In summary, this practice involves a review of real property title records for the property; a review of all public and agency records concerning compliance with environmental laws on the site and nearby properties; interviews with current and past owners, tenants, and neighbors concerning current and past uses and previous complaints concerning the property; and a site inspection by a competent environmental professional. The phase I assessment does not include any soil boring, monitoring well installation, or sample collection and analysis. Such activities are reserved for later investigations if evidence of possible contamination turns up from records, interviews, or observations during the site visit.

RCRA. The Resource Conservation and Recovery Act, 42 U.S.C. § 6901 *et seq.,* (RCRA) imposes a rigorous "cradle-to-grave" scheme that regulates hazardous wastes from generation to final disposal or destruction. The term "generator" is defined as any person, by site location, whose act or process produces hazardous waste that is identified or listed in the regulations. If a generator determines that its waste is "hazardous waste," it must notify the EPA and the state of its activity and obtain an EPA identification number. Hazardous wastes cannot be stored on-site for more than 90 days without a permit, and must be shipped to a facility that is authorized to treat or dispose of the wastes. Hazardous waste must properly containerized, labeled, and manifested prior to shipment off-site. There are severe civil and criminal penalties for regulatory violations and disposal of hazardous wastes at unauthorized locations.

Underground storage tanks (USTs) containing regulated substances, including petroleum products, are also subject to regulation under RCRA. New USTs must meet minimum federal standards. Existing USTs must be replaced or upgraded to specified standards that will prevent overfilling, spills, and leaks. Where spills or leaks have caused contamination of soils or groundwater with petroleum products, the owner or operator of the UST system must report and clean up the contamination under state supervision.

Other hazardous materials laws.   The Toxic Substance Control Act, 15 U.S.C. § 2601 et seq., (TSCA) regulates listed toxic substances, including polychlorinated biphenyls (PCBs), which were once widely used in electrical equipment and for other purposes.

Under the Federal Water Pollution Control Act, 33 U.S.C. § 1251 et seq., (also known as the Clean Water Act), virtually every discharge of a "pollutant" into surface or groundwaters is prohibited without a permit. Pollutants include dredged spoil, solid waste, incinerator residue, sewage, garbage, sewage sludge, munitions, chemical wastes, radioactive wastes, and other industrial, municipal, and agricultural wastes.

The Hazardous Materials Transportation Act, 49 U.S.C. § 5101 et seq., is mentioned because of the extensive list of hazardous materials subject to regulation under that act.

Three other features of the definition of hazardous materials laws deserve mention. First, besides the listed federal laws, this definition includes state and local laws that may impose other or stricter requirements than their federal counterparts. Second, the definition is significantly broader than mere statutes; regulations, policies, and administrative or judicial pronouncements are included. Third, the definition expressly includes any amendments or new regulatory requirements that may come into effect following the date of the Deed of Trust.

"Hazardous materials."   While the definition of hazardous materials focuses initially on petroleum products, lead-based paints, PCBs, asbestos, and other substances often found at multifamily residential sites, the definition is broad enough to cover any substance present that is subject to regulation and may cause harm to humans or the environment.

PARAGRAPH 18 AND COMMENTARY

(a) Except for matters covered by a written program of operations and maintenance approved in writing by Lender (an "O&M Program") or

matters described in Section 18(b), Borrower shall not cause or permit any of the following:

(1) *the presence, use, generation, release, treatment, processing, storage (including storage in above ground and underground storage tanks), handling, or disposal of any Hazardous Materials on or under the Mortgaged Property or any other property of Borrower that is adjacent to the Mortgaged Property;*

(2) *the transportation of any Hazardous Materials to, from, or across the Mortgaged Property;*

(3) *any occurrence or condition on the Mortgaged Property or any other property of Borrower that is adjacent to the Mortgaged Property, which occurrence or condition is or may be in violation of Hazardous Materials Laws; or*

(4) *any violation of or noncompliance with the terms of any Environmental Permit with respect to the Mortgaged Property or any property of Borrower that is adjacent to the Mortgaged Property.*

The matters described in clauses (1) through (4) above are referred to collectively in this Section 18 as "Prohibited Activities or Conditions."

Explanation

Lenders do not rely solely on government enforcement of environmental requirements to protect their interests in mortgaged property. The Deed of Trust requires the borrower to comply with all hazardous materials laws and environmental permits, and makes failure to do so an event of default. Moreover, these "prohibited activities or conditions" bar the presence of and any lawful and permitted activities involving hazardous materials on the mortgaged property, even if such presence or activity would not violate hazardous materials laws. The only exceptions to this broad prohibition are those activities that the lender may approve in a written operations and maintenance program.

(b) *Prohibited Activities and Conditions shall not include the safe and lawful use and storage of quantities of (1) pre-packaged supplies, cleaning materials and petroleum products customarily used in the operation and maintenance of comparable multifamily properties; (2) cleaning materials, personal grooming items and other items sold in pre-packaged containers for consumer use and used by tenants and occupants of residential dwelling units in the Mortgaged Property; and (3) petroleum products used in the operation and maintenance of motor vehicles from time to time located on the Mortgaged Property's park-*

ing areas, so long as all of the foregoing are used, stored, handled, transported and disposed of in compliance with Hazardous Materials Laws.

Explanation

Paragraph 18(b) provides a narrow exemption from the broad prohibition in paragraph 18(a), and constitutes an acknowledgment that many substances found at residential properties (e.g., cleaning products) contain hazardous materials such as chlorine and ammonia. The lender allows the presence of these categories of materials, provided they are handled in accordance with hazardous materials laws.

(c) *Borrower shall take all commercially reasonable actions (including the inclusion of appropriate provisions in any Leases executed after the date of this Instrument) to prevent its employees, agents, and contractors, and all tenants and other occupants from causing or permitting any Prohibited Activities or Conditions. Borrower shall not lease or allow the sublease or use of all or any portion of the Mortgaged Property to any tenant or subtenant for nonresidential use by any user that, in the ordinary course of its business, would cause or permit any Prohibited Activity or Condition.*

Explanation

The Deed of Trust requires the borrower to impose the same requirements concerning prohibited activities or conditions on its employees, agents, contractors, tenants and occupants.

(d) *If an O&M Program has been established with respect to Hazardous Materials, Borrower shall comply in a timely manner with, and cause all employees, agents, and contractors of Borrower and any other persons present on the Mortgaged Property to comply with the O&M Program. All costs of performance of Borrower's obligations under any O&M Program shall be paid by Borrower, and Lender's out-of-pocket costs incurred in connection with the monitoring and review of the O&M Program and Borrower's performance shall be paid by Borrower upon demand by Lender. Any such out-of-pocket costs of Lender which Borrower fails to pay promptly shall become an additional part of the Indebtedness as provided in Section 12.*

(e) *Borrower represents and warrants to Lender that, except as previously disclosed by Borrower to Lender in writing:*

(1) *Borrower has not at any time engaged in, caused or permitted any Prohibited Activities or Conditions;*

(2) to the best of Borrower's knowledge after reasonable and diligent inquiry, no Prohibited Activities or Conditions exist or have existed;

(3) except to the extent previously disclosed by Borrower to Lender in writing, the Mortgaged Property does not now contain any underground storage tanks, and, to the best of Borrower's knowledge after reasonable and diligent inquiry, the Mortgaged Property has not contained any underground storage tanks in the past. If there is an underground storage tank located on the Property which has been previously disclosed by Borrower to Lender in writing, that tank complies with all requirements of Hazardous Materials Laws;

(4) Borrower has complied with all Hazardous Materials Laws, including all requirements for notification regarding releases of Hazardous Materials. Without limiting the generality of the foregoing, Borrower has obtained all Environmental Permits required for the operation of the Mortgaged Property in accordance with Hazardous Materials Laws now in effect and all such Environmental Permits are in full force and effect;

(5) no event has occurred with respect to the Mortgaged Property that constitutes, or with the passing of time or the giving of notice would constitute, noncompliance with the terms of any Environmental Permit;

(6) there are no actions, suits, claims or proceedings pending or, to the best of Borrower's knowledge after reasonable and diligent inquiry, threatened that involve the Mortgaged Property and allege, arise out of, or relate to any Prohibited Activity or Condition; and

(7) Borrower has not received any complaint, order, notice of violation or other communication from any Governmental Authority with regard to air emissions, water discharges, noise emissions or Hazardous Materials, or any other environmental, health or safety matters affecting the Mortgaged Property or any other property of Borrower that is adjacent to the Mortgaged Property.

The representations and warranties in this Section 18 shall be continuing representations and warranties that shall be deemed to be made by Borrower throughout the term of the loan evidenced by the Note, until the Indebtedness has been paid in full.

Explanation

A borrower's representations and warranties concerning the environmental history of the mortgaged property are among the most important sources of information available to a lender. The Deed of Trust obligates the borrower to represent and warrant unequivocally, inter alia, that the borrower has not conducted any prohibited activities or conditions on the mortgaged property. The borrower is entitled to provide a written schedule of exceptions to these representations for known instances of noncompliance and other matters within the scope of paragraph 18(e). As to activities that occurred on the mortgaged property before the borrower owned it, (e.g., the presence of underground tanks), the borrower may qualify its representations based on actual knowledge, but only after conducting reasonable and diligent inquiry. The borrower could satisfy the necessary inquiry by following the ASTM standard discussed earlier in this section. Paragraph 18(e) requires that the borrower make these representations and warranties continuously throughout the term of the loan—which is not unreasonable, inasmuch as the borrower is in the best position to discover the relevant facts.

(f) *Borrower shall promptly notify Lender in writing upon the occurrence of any of the following events:*

   (1) *Borrower's discovery of any Prohibited Activity or Condition;*

   (2) *Borrower's receipt of or knowledge of any complaint, order, notice of violation or other communication from any Governmental Authority or other person with regard to present or future alleged Prohibited Activities or Conditions or any other environmental, health or safety matters affecting the Mortgaged Property or any other property of Borrower that is adjacent to the Mortgaged Property; and*

   (3) *any representation or warranty in this Section 18 becomes untrue after the date of this Agreement.*

Any such notice given by Borrower shall not relieve Borrower of, or result in a waiver of, any obligation under this Instrument, the Note, or any other Loan Document.

Explanation

Paragraph 18(f) of the Deed of Trust places the burden on the borrower to remain abreast of, and report to the lender, any developments that may result in a governmental enforcement action or require some cleanup activity. The borrower's compliance with this reporting obligation does not relieve him of other obligations in the loan documents.

(g) *Borrower shall pay promptly the costs of any environmental inspections, tests or audits (**"Environmental Inspections"**) required by Lender in*

connection with any foreclosure or deed in lieu of foreclosure, or as a condition of Lender's consent to any Transfer under Section 21, or required by Lender following a reasonable determination by Lender that Prohibited Activities or Conditions may exist. Any such costs incurred by Lender (including the fees and out-of-pocket costs of attorneys and technical consultants whether incurred in connection with any judicial or administrative process or otherwise) which Borrower fails to pay promptly shall become an additional part of the Indebtedness as provided in Section 12. The results of all Environmental Inspections made by Lender shall at all times remain the property of Lender and Lender shall have no obligation to disclose or otherwise make available to Borrower or any other party such results or any other information obtained by Lender in connection with its Environmental Inspections. Lender hereby reserves the right, and Borrower hereby expressly authorizes Lender, to make available to any party, including any prospective bidder at a foreclosure sale of the Mortgaged Property, the results of any Environmental Inspections made by Lender with respect to the Mortgaged Property. Borrower consents to Lender notifying any party (either as part of a notice of sale or otherwise) of the results of any of Lender's Environmental Inspections. Borrower acknowledges that Lender cannot control or otherwise assure the truthfulness or accuracy of the results of any of its Environmental Inspections and that the release of such results to prospective bidders at a foreclosure sale of the Mortgaged Property may have a material and adverse effect upon the amount which a party may bid at such sale. Borrower agrees that Lender shall have no liability whatsoever as a result of delivering the results of any of its Environmental Inspections to any third party, and Borrower hereby releases and forever discharges Lender from any and all claims, damages, or causes of action, arising out of, connected with or incidental to the results of, the delivery of any of Lender's Environmental Inspections.

Explanation

Despite the protections for secured parties, no lender should foreclose on and take title to mortgaged property before satisfying itself that the property remains free of contamination that could lead to CERCLA liability. Therefore, paragraph 18(g) reserves to the lender the right to order an environmental assessment of the mortgaged property—to be conducted at the borrower's expense—when the mortgaged property is subject to foreclosure or transfer of title, or at any time the lender reasonably believes that contamination may be present. The Deed of Trust also permits the lender to choose the consultants to perform such assessments and to control the scope and conduct of such assessments.

Further, paragraph 18(g) reserves to the lender the right to withhold or disclose the information generated as the lender sees fit to protect its interests, whether or not the borrower objects. The lender may wish to have its lawyers direct such assessments and protect the work product from disclosure to third parties under the attorney-client and attorney work product privileges. Granting the borrower the right to the information might destroy these privileges and lead to disclosure of the information to other third parties. In contrast, the Deed of Trust authorizes the lender to disclose any information discovered to any governmental agency to which reports must be made, or to prospective buyers, even if the borrower objects because its interest will be adversely affected.

(h) *If any investigation, site monitoring, containment, clean-up, restoration or other remedial work* (**"Remedial Work"**) *is necessary to comply with any Hazardous Materials Law or order of any Governmental Authority that has or acquires jurisdiction over the Mortgaged Property or the use, operation or improvement of the Mortgaged Property under any Hazardous Materials Law, Borrower shall, by the earlier of (1) the applicable deadline required by Hazardous Materials Law or (2) 30 days after notice from Lender demanding such action, begin performing the Remedial Work, and thereafter diligently prosecute it to completion, and shall in any event complete the work by the time required by applicable Hazardous Materials Law. If Borrower fails to begin on a timely basis or diligently prosecute any required Remedial Work, Lender may, at its option, cause the Remedial Work to be completed, in which case Borrower shall reimburse Lender on demand for the cost of doing so. Any reimbursement due from Borrower to Lender shall become part of the Indebtedness as provided in Section 12.*

Explanation

Paragraph 18(h) of the Deed of Trust authorizes the lender to require the borrower to undertake and complete "remedial work" to comply not only with governmental cleanup orders, but also with the lender's directions to correct noncompliance problems on the mortgaged property. The Deed of Trust reserves the latter right because the lender cannot rely on any governmental authority to require the borrower to conduct needed remedial actions, or to prosecute an effective enforcement action if the borrower fails to comply. Alternatively, if the borrower fails to act, paragraph 18 of the Deed of Trust permits the lender to perform the cleanup at the borrower's expense, and to add the cost to the mortgage indebtedness. *See supra* Section 12.

(i) *Borrower shall cooperate with any inquiry by any Governmental Authority and shall comply with any governmental or judicial order which arises from any alleged Prohibited Activity or Condition.*

(j) *Borrower shall indemnify, hold harmless and defend (i) Lender, (ii) any prior owner or holder of the Note, (iii) the Loan Servicer, (iv) any prior Loan Servicer, (v) the officers, directors, shareholders, partners, employees and trustees of any of the foregoing, and (vi) the heirs, legal representatives, successors and assigns of each of the foregoing (collectively, the* **"Indemnitees")** *from and against all proceedings, claims, damages, penalties and costs (whether initiated or sought by Governmental Authorities or private parties), including fees and out-of-pocket expenses of attorneys and expert witnesses, investigatory fees, and remediation costs, whether incurred in connection with any judicial or administrative process or otherwise, arising directly or indirectly from any of the following:*

(1) *any breach of any representation or warranty of Borrower in this Section 18;*

(2) *any failure by Borrower to perform any of its obligations under this Section 18;*

(3) *the existence or alleged existence of any Prohibited Activity or Condition;*

(4) *the presence or alleged presence of Hazardous Materials on or under the Mortgaged Property or any property of Borrower that is adjacent to the Mortgaged Property; and*

(5) *the actual or alleged violation of any Hazardous Materials Law.*

(k) *Counsel selected by Borrower to defend Indemnitees shall be subject to the approval of those Indemnitees. However, any Indemnitee may elect to defend any claim or legal or administrative proceeding at the Borrower's expense.*

(l) *Borrower shall not, without the prior written consent of those Indemnitees who are named as parties to a claim or legal or administrative proceeding (a* **"Claim"**), *settle or compromise the Claim if the settlement (1) results in the entry of any judgment that does not include as an unconditional term the delivery by the claimant or plaintiff to Lender of a written release of those Indemnitees, satisfactory in form and substance to Lender; or (2) may materially and adversely affect Lender, as determined by Lender in its discretion.*

(m) Lender agrees that the indemnity under this Section 18 shall be limited to the assets of Borrower and Lender shall not seek to recover any deficiency from any natural persons who are general partners of Borrower.

(n) Borrower shall, at its own cost and expense, do all of the following:

    (1) pay or satisfy any judgment or decree that may be entered against any Indemnitee or Indemnitees in any legal or administrative proceeding incident to any matters against which Indemnitees are entitled to be indemnified under this Section 18;

    (2) reimburse Indemnitees for any expenses paid or incurred in connection with any matters against which Indemnitees are entitled to be indemnified under this Section 18; and

    (3) reimburse Indemnitees for any and all expenses, including fees and out-of-pocket expenses of attorneys and expert witnesses, paid or incurred in connection with the enforcement by Indemnitees of their rights under this Section 18, or in monitoring and participating in any legal or administrative proceeding.

(o) In any circumstances in which the indemnity under this Section 18 applies, Lender may employ its own legal counsel and consultants to prosecute, defend or negotiate any claim or legal or administrative proceeding and Lender, with the prior written consent of Borrower (which shall not be unreasonably withheld, delayed or conditioned), may settle or compromise any action or legal or administrative proceeding. Borrower shall reimburse Lender upon demand for all costs and expenses incurred by Lender, including all costs of settlements entered into in good faith, and the fees and out-of-pocket expenses of such attorneys and consultants.

(p) The provisions of this Section 18 shall be in addition to any and all other obligations and liabilities that Borrower may have under applicable law or under other Loan Documents, and each Indemnitee shall be entitled to indemnification under this Section 18 without regard to whether Lender or that Indemnitee has exercised any rights against the Mortgaged Property or any other security, pursued any rights against any guarantor, or pursued any other rights available under the Loan Documents or applicable law. If Borrower consists of more than one person or entity, the obligation of those persons or entities to indemnify the Indemnitees under this Section 18 shall be joint and several. The obligation of Borrower to indemnify the Indemnitees under this Section 18 shall survive any repayment or discharge of the Indebtedness, any foreclosure proceeding, any foreclosure sale, any delivery of any deed in lieu of foreclosure, and any release of record of the lien of this Instrument.

Explanation

Environmental provisions in real estate and financial documents commonly include indemnity rights. Current and past property owners and tenants, as well as their lenders, have been subjected to lawsuits seeking cleanup actions. In the liability phase of such litigation, a defendant may be unable to defend by arguing that another party is or should be entirely responsible for the contamination. Instead, it is a common occurrence that a number of parties will be "caught in the net" of liability as potentially responsible parties (PRPs), and will incur large litigation expenses. In the relief or damages phase of the case, if the case is not settled first, the share of liability to be borne by each party will be established. Also, while the governmental cleanup action is threatened or pending, the lender may undertake some cleanup action, either voluntarily or involuntarily. The indemnity provisions appearing in paragraph 18 of the Deed of Trust enable the lender to recover these costs directly from the borrower.

Property and Liability Insurance

Borrower shall keep the Improvements insured at all times against such hazards as Lender may from time to time require, which insurance shall include but not be limited to coverage against loss by fire and allied perils, general boiler and machinery coverage, and business income coverage. Lender's insurance requirements may change from time to time throughout the term of the Indebtedness. If Lender so requires, such insurance shall also include sinkhole insurance, mine subsidence insurance, earthquake insurance, and, if the Mortgaged Property does not conform to applicable zoning or land use laws, building ordinance or law coverage. If any of the Improvements is located in an area identified by the Federal Emergency Management Agency (or any successor to that agency) as an area having special flood hazards, and if flood insurance is available in that area, Borrower shall insure such Improvements against loss by flood.

All premiums on insurance policies required under Section 19(a) shall be paid in the manner provided in Section 7, unless Lender has designated in writing another method of payment. All such policies shall also be in a form approved by Lender. All policies of property damage insurance shall include a non-contributing, non-reporting mortgage clause in favor of, and in a form approved by, Lender. Lender shall have the right to hold the original policies or duplicate original policies of all insurance required by Section 19(a). Borrower shall promptly deliver to Lender a copy of all renewal and other notices received by Borrower with respect to the policies and all receipts for paid premiums. At

107

least 30 days prior to the expiration date of a policy, Borrower shall deliver to Lender the original (or a duplicate original) of a renewal policy in form satisfactory to Lender.

Borrower shall maintain at all times commercial general liability insurance, workers' compensation insurance and such other liability, errors and omissions and fidelity insurance coverages as Lender may from time to time require.

All insurance policies and renewals of insurance policies required by this Section 19 shall be in such amounts and for such periods as Lender may from time to time require, and shall be issued by insurance companies satisfactory to Lender.

Borrower shall comply with all insurance requirements and shall not permit any condition to exist on the Mortgaged Property that would invalidate any part of any insurance coverage that this Instrument requires Borrower to maintain.

In the event of loss, Borrower shall give immediate written notice to the insurance carrier and to Lender. Borrower hereby authorizes and appoints Lender as attorney-in-fact for Borrower to make proof of loss, to adjust and compromise any claims under policies of property damage insurance, to appear in and prosecute any action arising from such property damage insurance policies, to collect and receive the proceeds of property damage insurance, and to deduct from such proceeds Lender's expenses incurred in the collection of such proceeds. This power of attorney is coupled with an interest and therefore is irrevocable. However, nothing contained in this Section 19 shall require Lender to incur any expense or take any action. Lender may, at Lender's option, (1) hold the balance of such proceeds to be used to reimburse Borrower for the cost of restoring and repairing the Mortgaged Property to the equivalent of its original condition or to a condition approved by Lender (the "Restoration"), or (2) apply the balance of such proceeds to the payment of the Indebtedness, whether or not then due. To the extent Lender determines to apply insurance proceeds to Restoration, Lender shall do so in accordance with Lender's then-current policies relating to the restoration of casualty damage on similar multifamily properties.

Lender shall not exercise its option to apply insurance proceeds to the payment of the Indebtedness if all of the following conditions are met: (1) no Event of Default (or any event which, with the giving of notice or the passage of time, or both, would constitute an Event of Default) has occurred and is continuing; (2) Lender determines, in its discretion, that there will be sufficient funds to complete the Restoration; (3) Lender determines, in its discretion, that the rental income from the Mortgaged Property after completion of the Restoration will be sufficient to meet all operating costs and other ex-

penses, Imposition Deposits, deposits to reserves and loan repayment obligations relating to the Mortgaged Property; (4) Lender determines, in its discretion, that the Restoration will be completed before the earlier of (A) one year before the maturity date of the Note or (B) one year after the date of the loss or casualty; and (5) upon Lender's request, Borrower provides Lender evidence of the availability during and after the Restoration of the insurance required to be maintained by Borrower pursuant to this Section 19.

If the Mortgaged Property is sold at a foreclosure sale or Lender acquires title to the Mortgaged Property, Lender shall automatically succeed to all rights of Borrower in and to any insurance policies and unearned insurance premiums and in and to the proceeds resulting from any damage to the Mortgaged Property prior to such sale or acquisition.

Explanation

Casualty insurance. Adequate casualty insurance coverage is essential to a lender; without it, a loss could easily make the property's value inadequate to cover the mortgage debt. When the mortgage requires the borrower to carry insurance (as in paragraph 19 of the Deed of Trust), or when the lender is shown as an insured on the policy, the courts regard the insurance proceeds as a form of substitute collateral for the real estate. *See* RESTATEMENT (THIRD) OF PROPERTY: MORTGAGES § 4.7 (1997); San Roman v. Atlantic Mutual Ins. Co., 250 A.D.2d 585 (N.Y. 1998) (lender could claim insurance proceeds despite the fact that the loan was nonrecourse and that lender was not shown on the policy as a loss payee).

The Deed of Trust is, of course, highly pro-lender, permitting the lender to determine the hazards to be covered, the amount of coverage, and the policy form. Virtually all modern casualty insurance employs the "standard mortgage clause" (also called the "union mortgage clause"), which preserves the lender's insurance coverage despite any act or neglect of the mortgagor or owner. *See* John W. Steinmetz et al., *The Standard Mortgage Clause in Property Insurance Policies*, 33 TORT & INS. L.J. 81 (1997); Neil J. Lehto, *The Standard Mortgage Clause under Attack: The Lender's Insurance Claim When a Borrower Commits Arson*, 66 U. DET. L. REV. 603 (1989). Thus, although the Deed of Trust provides that the borrower "shall not permit any condition to exist on the Mortgaged Property that would invalidate any part of any insurance coverage," if such a condition existed it would not affect the lender's insurance coverage.

However, several cases have held that the standard mortgage clause assures the lender of coverage only for the real estate, and not for associated *personal* property, even if the insurance itself covers such property. *See, e.g.,* General Electric Credit Corp. v. Aetna Casualty & Surety Co., 263 A.2d 448 (Pa. 1970). Lenders should take care to ensure that their personal property coverage will not be affected by the borrower's breach of policy conditions.

Restoration after loss.   When a loss to mortgaged property occurs and the insurance company makes a payment under its policy, a heated controversy often arises: Can the borrower use the policy proceeds for restoration of the property, or is the lender entitled to insist that the proceeds be applied to pay down or satisfy the mortgage loan instead? In theory, applying the proceeds toward the loan balance is economically beneficial to the borrower, but it may compel it to go into the mortgage market and refinance—negotiating what is, in effect, a construction loan under adverse market conditions.

If the mortgage provides that the lender has the option to apply the funds to the loan balance, as does paragraph 19 of the Deed of Trust, the courts nearly always uphold that provision. Some cases allow the lender to take an amount up to the full mortgage balance. *See* City of Chicago v. Salinger, 52 N.E.2d 184 (Ill. 1943). Others, representing a minority view, limit the lender to the amount needed to compensate for the impairment of security it has suffered from the loss. *See* Harwell v. Georgia Power Co. 298 S.E.2d 498 (Ga. 1983). The Restatement takes the view that the lender has a duty to permit use of the funds for restoration of the property if restoration is reasonably feasible and will return the property to its value at the time the loan was made. *See* RESTATEMENT (THIRD) OF PROPERTY: MORTGAGES § 4.7(b). However, case authority supporting this view is meager. *See* Schoolcraft v. Ross, 146 Cal. Rptr. 57 (Cal. Ct. App. 1978).

Paragraph 19 of the Deed of Trust is relatively generous to borrowers in this respect. It requires the lender to allow use of the insurance proceeds for restoration if the loan is not in default, the funds are sufficient to complete the restoration, the project will generate sufficient income after restoration to cover the debt service and all operating expenses, and the restoration can be completed within a year from the date of the loss. These are all reasonable conditions, and courts would almost certainly uphold them. There is one further limitation: The lender need not release the insurance proceeds for restoration if the loan will mature within one year after the restoration is completed. The rationale for this limitation is that the lender should not have to endure the trouble of restoration if the loan has only one year or less to maturity.

Condemnation

Borrower shall promptly notify Lender of any action or proceeding relating to any condemnation or other taking, or conveyance in lieu thereof, of all or any part of the Mortgaged Property, whether direct or indirect (a "Condemnation"). Borrower shall appear in and prosecute or defend any action or proceeding relating to any Condemnation unless otherwise directed by Lender in writing. Borrower authorizes and appoints Lender as attorney-in-fact for Borrower to commence, appear in and prosecute, in Lender's or Borrower's name, any action or proceeding relating to any Condemnation and to settle or compromise any claim in connection with any Condemnation. This power of attorney is coupled with an interest and therefore is irrevocable. However, nothing contained in this Section 20 shall require Lender to incur any expense or take any action. Borrower hereby transfers and assigns to Lender all right, title and interest of Borrower in and to any award or payment with respect to (i) any Condemnation, or any conveyance in lieu of Condemnation, and (ii) any damage to the Mortgaged Property caused by governmental action that does not result in a Condemnation.

Lender may apply such awards or proceeds, after the deduction of Lender's expenses incurred in the collection of such amounts, at Lender's option, to the restoration or repair of the Mortgaged Property or to the payment of the Indebtedness, with the balance, if any, to Borrower. Unless Lender otherwise agrees in writing, any application of any awards or proceeds to the Indebtedness shall not extend or postpone the due date of any monthly install-

ments referred to in the Note, Section 7 of this Instrument or any Collateral Agreement, or change the amount of such installments. Borrower agrees to execute such further evidence of assignment of any awards or proceeds as Lender may require.

Explanation

Eminent domain awards. The proceeds of an eminent domain award are similar to casualty insurance proceeds, and are regarded as a substitute res to which the mortgage lien attaches. *See* G. NELSON & D. WHITMAN, REAL ESTATE FINANCE LAW § 4.12 (3d ed. 1993); Harold D. Teague, *Condemnation of Mortgaged Property*, 44 Tex. L. Rev. 1535 (1966). Paragraph 20 of the Deed of Trust implements this principle.

Paragraph 19 permits the lender to use the proceeds for restoration of the property. However, there is a major difference between the treatment of eminent domain awards here and the treatment of casualty insurance proceeds in paragraph 19. When eminent domain awards are received, the lender has the absolute discretion as to whether to apply them toward the loan balance or toward restoration of the property. There is no affirmative duty on the lender's part to permit use of the funds for restoration, even if restoration is feasible. The reason for the difference is that when a condemnation occurs, unlike an insured casualty, at least part of the property is simply gone and literally cannot be restored. It is true that in some cases the taking may be of a minor part of the property, and it may be possible to restore the property's value to its pre-taking level by applying the eminent domain award. But these instances are probably rare, so borrowers are unlikely to complain much about the lender having discretion to allocate the award.

Transfers of the Mortgaged Property or Interests in Borrower

(a) The occurrence of any of the following events shall constitute an Event of Default under this Instrument:

   (1) a Transfer of all or any part of the Mortgaged Property or any interest in the Mortgaged Property;

   (2) a Transfer of a Controlling Interest in Borrower;

   (3) a Transfer of a Controlling Interest in any entity which owns, directly or indirectly through one or more intermediate entities, a Controlling Interest in Borrower;

   (4) a Transfer of all or any part of Key Principal's ownership interests (other than limited partnership interests) in Borrower, or in any other entity which owns, directly or indirectly through one or more intermediate entities, an ownership interest in Borrower;

   (5) if Key Principal is an entity, (A) a Transfer of a Controlling Interest in Key Principal, or (B) a Transfer of a Controlling Interest in any entity which owns, directly or indirectly through one or more intermediate entities, a Controlling Interest in Key Principal;

   (6) if Borrower or Key Principal is a trust, the termination or revocation of such trust; and

   (7) a conversion of Borrower from one type of legal entity into another type of legal entity, whether or not there is a Transfer.

Lender shall not be required to demonstrate any actual impairment of its security or any increased risk of default in order to exercise any of its remedies with respect to an Event of Default under this Section 21.

(b) *The occurrence of any of the following events shall not constitute an Event of Default under this Instrument, notwithstanding any provision of Section 21(a) to the contrary:*

(1) *a Transfer to which Lender has consented;*

(2) *a Transfer that occurs by devise, descent, or by operation of law upon the death of a natural person;*

(3) *the grant of a leasehold interest in an individual dwelling unit for a term of two years or less not containing an option to purchase;*

(4) *a Transfer of obsolete or worn out Personalty or Fixtures that are contemporaneously replaced by items of equal or better function and quality, which are free of liens, encumbrances and security interests other than those created by the Loan Documents or consented to by Lender;*

(5) *the grant of an easement, if before the grant Lender determines that the easement will not materially affect the operation or value of the Mortgaged Property or Lender's interest in the Mortgaged Property, and Borrower pays to Lender, upon demand, all costs and expenses incurred by Lender in connection with reviewing Borrower's request; and*

(6) *the creation of a tax lien or a mechanic's, materialman's or judgment lien against the Mortgaged Property which is bonded off, released of record or otherwise remedied to Lender's satisfaction within 30 days of the date of creation.*

(c) *Lender shall consent, without any adjustment to the rate at which the Indebtedness secured by this Instrument bears interest or to any other economic terms of the Indebtedness, to a Transfer that would otherwise violate this Section 21 if, prior to the Transfer, Borrower has satisfied each of the following requirements:*

(1) *the submission to Lender of all information required by Lender to make the determination required by this Section 21(c);*

(2) *the absence of any Event of Default;*

(3) *the transferee meets all of the eligibility, credit, management and other standards (including any standards with respect to previous relationships between Lender and the transferee and the organization of the transferee) customarily applied by Lender at the time of the*

proposed Transfer to the approval of borrowers in connection with the origination or purchase of similar mortgages, deeds of trust or deeds to secure debt on multifamily properties;

(4) the Mortgaged Property, at the time of the proposed Transfer, meets all standards as to its physical condition that are customarily applied by Lender at the time of the proposed Transfer to the approval of properties in connection with the origination or purchase of similar mortgages on multifamily properties;

(5) in the case of a Transfer of all or any part of the Mortgaged Property, or direct or indirect ownership interests in Borrower or Key Principal (if an entity), if transferor or any other person has obligations under any Loan Document, the execution by the transferee or one or more individuals or entities acceptable to Lender of an assumption agreement (including, if applicable, an Acknowledgement and Agreement of Key Principal to Personal Liability for Exceptions to Non-Recourse Liability) that is acceptable to Lender and that, among other things, requires the transferee to perform all obligations of transferor or such person set forth in such Loan Document, and may require that the transferee comply with any provisions of this Instrument or any other Loan Document which previously may have been waived by Lender;

(6) if a guaranty has been executed and delivered in connection with the Note, this Instrument or any of the other Loan Documents, the Borrower causes one or more individuals or entities acceptable to Lender to execute and deliver to Lender a guaranty in a form acceptable to Lender; and

(7) Lender's receipt of all of the following:

(A) a non-refundable review fee in the amount of $3,000 and a transfer fee equal to 1 percent of the outstanding Indebtedness immediately prior to the Transfer.

(B) In addition, Borrower shall be required to reimburse Lender for all of Lender's out-of-pocket costs (including reasonable attorneys' fees) incurred in reviewing the Transfer request, to the extent such expenses exceed $3,000.

(d) For purposes of this Section, the following terms shall have the meanings set forth below:

(1) **"Initial Owners"** means, with respect to Borrower or any other entity, the persons or entities who on the date of the Note own in the aggregate 100% of the ownership interests in Borrower or that entity.

(2) A Transfer of a **"Controlling Interest"** shall mean, with respect to any entity, the following:

(i) if such entity is a general partnership or a joint venture, a Transfer of any general partnership interest or joint venture interest which would cause the Initial Owners to own less than 51% of all general partnership or joint venture interests in such entity;

(ii) if such entity is a limited partnership, a Transfer of any general partnership interest;

(iii) if such entity is a limited liability company or a limited liability partnership, a Transfer of any membership or other ownership interest which would cause the Initial Owners to own less than 51% of all membership or other ownership interests in such entity;

(iv) if such entity is a corporation (other than a Publicly-Held Corporation) with only one class of voting stock, a Transfer of any voting stock which would cause the Initial Owners to own less than 51% of voting stock in such corporation;

(v) if such entity is a corporation (other than a Publicly-Held Corporation) with more than one class of voting stock, a Transfer of any voting stock which would cause the Initial Owners to own less than a sufficient number of shares of voting stock having the power to elect the majority of directors of such corporation; and

(vi) if such entity is a trust, the removal, appointment or substitution of a trustee of such trust other than (A) in the case of a land trust, or (B) if the trustee of such trust after such removal, appointment or substitution is a trustee identified in the trust agreement approved by Lender.

(3) **"Publicly-Held Corporation"** shall mean a corporation the outstanding voting stock of which is registered under Section 12(b) or 12(g) of the Securities and Exchange Act of 1934, as amended.

Explanation

The lender's interest in the borrower's identity. When a lender makes a loan to a specific borrower that is secured by a mortgage on a specific real estate project, the lender does so after evaluating the borrower's creditworthiness, reputation, and experience and the value of the real estate being pledged. Consequently, it is important to the lender that during the term of the loan, the borrowing entity—and ultimately, the people who control the borrowing entity and subentities—does not change without the lender's consent, that the borrowing entity retains a controlling interest in the mortgaged property, and that there is no change in the identity of any key persons in control of the borrowing entity.

One way for the lender to obtain such assurance is to prohibit any transfers of the mortgaged property or of any controlling interests in the borrowing entity and subentities, as set forth in Paragraph 21(a) of the Deed of Trust. The exceptions listed in Paragraph 21(b) are ones that borrowers commonly request and that lenders typically can accept, as they do not impinge upon the basic protections that a lender seeks to achieve using a "due-on-sale" provision. Paragraph 21(c) relates to the type of transfers that potentially may be of concern to lenders, but provides a procedure by which the borrower can seek the lender's consent to the transfer, including the payment of a specified nonrefundable review fee, a transfer fee, and reimbursement of the lender's out-of-pocket expenses incurred in reviewing the transfer request.

The enforceability of due-on-sale clauses.   Congress enacted the Garn–St. Germain Depository Institutions Act, 12 U.S.C. § 1701 *et seq.*, in 1982. The act provides that a lender's actions relating to due-on-sale situations are governed by the terms of the loan documents. The act clarified that due-on-sale clauses are enforceable, notwithstanding state law to the contrary. Prior to this act, the enforcement of due-on-sale clauses was less certain, particularly in cases where lenders sought to enforce a due-on-sale clause to prevent a sale of the mortgaged property and an assumption of the mortgage loan by the purchaser. Courts in numerous states denied enforcement of a due-on-sale clause in such circumstances unless the lender could show that its mortgage lien was impaired by the sale, or that the sale increased the risk of the borrower's default. *See, e.g.,* Wellenkamp v. Bank of America, 582 P.2d 970, 977 (Cal. 1978). The act applies to both residential and commercial loans, with nine exceptions in the residential context. 12 U.S.C. § 1701j-3(d).

To what extent may the lender condition its consent to sale or transfer?
Loan documents sometimes simply provide that the borrower may not sell the mortgaged property without the lender's consent. When a borrower comes to the lender seeking consent to a proposed sale, the lender sometimes conditions its consent upon receiving additional collateral. This was the situation in *Destin Savings Bank v. Summerhouse of FWB, Inc.,* 579 So. 2d 232 (Fla. Dist. Ct. App. 1991), where the court held that the lender could condition its consent to the sale on the borrower

providing additional collateral. In *Destin Savings*, Anderson (president of Summerhouse of FWB) received a commercial loan from Destin Savings to enable him to develop a restaurant. The mortgage and security agreement prohibited any sale, conveyance, transfer, lease, or encumbrance without the mortgagee's written consent, and declared any transfer without consent to be void. The mortgage also provided that an event of default would occur if any other party obtained an interest in all or any part of the mortgaged property, thus authorizing the mortgagee to declare the outstanding principal and accrued interest due and payable immediately. In 1989, without the mortgagee's consent, Anderson entered into a sales contract for the restaurant with Hobbs. After Anderson submitted Hobbs's financial statements to Destin Savings for their approval, Destin Savings conditioned its consent to Hobbs's assumption of the mortgage upon Hobbs's agreement to pledge a $100,000 certificate of deposit to Destin Savings or to grant a second mortgage on his home to Destin Savings. Hobbs refused, and Anderson and Hobbs completed the sale without obtaining Destin's approval. Summerhouse and Hobbs filed complaints against Destin Savings seeking a declaration as to their rights under the mortgage agreement, including a judgment regarding Destin's demand for additional collateral. The circuit court applied a reasonableness standard to Destin's exercise of the due-on-sale clause, concluded that Destin's conditions were unreasonable, and allowed the assumption. The appellate court reversed, holding that the Garn Act applied in commercial transactions and that under the act, Destin's actions were consistent with the terms of the loan documents. Because the mortgage did not include language indicating that Destin's consent would not be unreasonably withheld, the court refused to impose a reasonableness standard on Destin as mortgagee. *Id.* at 237. The court did not apply the Restatement of Property to the facts of the case.

In some cases, loan documents provide that the lender will not "unreasonably" withhold consent to a sale. A question then arises as to what constitutes "reasonable" grounds for withholding consent. For example, can the lender condition its consent on an increase in the interest rate? One line of cases has ruled that a lender can so condition its consent. *See, e.g.*, Torgerson-Forstrom H.I. of Willmar, Inc. v. Olmstead Federal Savings & Loan Ass'n, 339 N.W.2d 901, 904 (Minn. 1983) (due-on-sale clause serves dual purpose: (i) protection of the lender's security interest in the mortgaged property (issues of the creditworthiness and expertise of the proposed new owner of the property) and (ii) protection of the lender's position in the money market (keeping its investments at market rates)); Western Life Insurance Co. v. McPherson K.M.P., 702 F. Supp 836 (D. Kan. 1988). *See also* Rustic Hills Shopping Plaza, Inc. v. Columbia Savings & Loan Ass'n, 661 P.2d 254 (Col. 1983) (conditioning consent to sale on increasing interest rate from 7 to 15 percent was not unconscionable conduct or unreasonable restraint on alienation, when interest rates on new loan would have been approximately 18 to 19 percent).

Negotiation of the due-on-sale clause.   Because courts will freely enforce the terms of loan documents with respect to due-on-sale clauses, it is important for lenders and borrowers to carefully negotiate the terms of the due-on-sale provision. If the lender would be willing to consent to a sale if it can condition such consent on requiring additional collateral, charging a fee, or increasing the interest rate, then the borrower should insist that the loan documents expressly so provide. Because paragraph 21 of the Deed of Trust provides what appears to be a reasonable (as opposed to unconscionable) fee for the lender's consent (1 percent), there is little doubt as to its enforceability. The Deed of Trust also wisely provides that the lender need not show impairment of the mortgage as the basis for exercise of the due-on-sale clause. As the court stated in *Western Life Insurance Co. v. McPherson,* "the parties to a loan contract can limit a lender's right to exercise a due-on-sale clause to situations when a change in the ownership would impair the lender's security," but a clause that merely provides that the lender will not unreasonably withhold consent does not require that the lender demonstrate impairment of security. *Western Life,* 702 F. Supp. at 842.

Events of Default

The occurrence of any one or more of the following shall constitute an Event of Default under this Instrument:

Explanation

Threats to the lender's interests. As a practical matter, the lender's ability to accelerate the maturity of the mortgage debt and institute foreclosure proceedings is a function of the mortgage contract. Accordingly, paragraph 22 of the Deed of Trust defines the existence of an "event of default" with regard to the occurrence of events or circumstances that would tend to threaten (a) the lender's prospect of payment on the mortgage debt in a timely fashion, (b) the physical integrity, prudent management, or financial value of the mortgaged property, or (c) the lender's ability to exercise its default remedies in a prompt and effective fashion following default.

(a)   any failure by Borrower to pay or deposit when due any amount required by the Note, this Instrument or any other Loan Document;

Explanation

Monetary defaults.   The lender's most significant ex ante expectation is that the borrower will repay the mortgage indebtedness in accordance with its terms. Thus, paragraph 22(a) of the Deed of Trust provides that the borrower's failure to pay in a timely fashion justifies the lender's decision to accelerate the maturity of the mortgage debt pursuant to paragraph 43. Furthermore, paragraph 22(a) also obligates the borrower to pay in a timely fashion certain other obligations integrally related to the preservation of the lender's mortgage lien, including real estate taxes (*see supra* Section 15) and casualty insurance premiums (*see supra* Section 19). The borrower's failure to pay these sums on a timely basis justifies the lender's decision to accelerate the maturity of the debt.

As a threshold matter, what constitutes "timely" payment is a function of the provisions of the note and other loan documents. Thus, as a starting point, a borrower's failure to pay within the time specified by the express language of the note generally would justify the lender's decision to declare a default and accelerate the maturity of the debt.

Nevertheless, lenders must be cautious about the frequent or regular acceptance of late payments. Where a lender has established a course of dealing with a particular borrower, under which it has accepted late payments on more than an occasional basis, many courts have freely sustained borrower challenges to acceleration of the debt. Often, these courts have concluded that the lender's acceptance of late payments resulted in a waiver of the right to demand strict compliance with the express language of the debt instrument, or estopped the lender from accelerating the debt before first giving notice to the borrower that it would insist upon timely payment in the future. *See, e.g.*, Miller v. Uhrick, 706 P.2d 739 (Ariz. App. 1985); Dad's Properties, Inc. v. Lucas, 545 So. 2d 926 (Fla. Dist. Ct. App. 1989); Edwards v. Smith, 322 S.W.2d 770 (Mo. 1959); Rosselot v. Heimbrock, 561 N.E.2d 555 (Ohio App. 1988); Fairfield Financial Group, Inc. v. Gawerc, 814 S.W.2d 204 (Tex. App. 1991). Accordingly, on any occasion that a lender elects to accept payment of an installment on the mortgage debt in an untimely fashion, that lender should issue a written notice to the borrower, advising that its acceptance of the payment does not modify the terms of the loan documents and does not waive the lender's ability to demand strict compliance with the express terms of those loan documents in the future.

(b) *any failure by Borrower to maintain the insurance coverage required by Section 19;*

Explanation

Insurance coverage.   A borrower's failure to insure the mortgaged premises adequately could have devastating consequences for the lender—

especially in the context of a nonrecourse loan—if a casualty damages or destroys the premises. Paragraph 22(b) of the Deed of Trust discourages the borrower's failure to insure the mortgaged premises by allowing the lender to use such failure as a basis for accelerating the mortgage debt.

The declaration of an event of default under paragraph 22(b) should be extremely rare. As is typical in mortgage loan documentation, paragraph 19(b) requires the borrower to provide evidence of policy renewal to the lender 30 days prior to the policy's expiration. Thus, the prudent lender who fails to receive such evidence in a timely fashion should have ample time and opportunity to secure substitute coverage or take adequate steps to ensure the borrower's renewal of the existing policy. For further explanation, see Section 19.

(c)   *any failure by Borrower to comply with the provisions of Section 33;*

Explanation

Single-asset real estate.   The Bankruptcy Code provides a significant constraint upon a lender's ability to enforce its default remedies following the borrower's default. The borrower's bankruptcy petition effects an automatic stay against creditor enforcement activity (11 U.S.C. § 362(a)), thereby preventing the lender from pursuing its state law collection remedies without relief granted by the bankruptcy court.

Single-asset real estate entities, of course, are perhaps not the traditional bankrupt "debtor" that Congress envisioned in enacting the Bankruptcy Code. Single-asset real estate entities typically have only one major creditor—the mortgage lender. To the extent that a single-asset real estate borrower does have trade creditors, those creditors will tend to hold claims that are in percentage terms relatively insignificant compared with the mortgage debt. As a result, many have questioned whether single-asset real estate entities should receive the benefit of bankruptcy protection at all. *See, e.g.,* Shannon C. Bogle, *Bonner Mall and Single-Asset Real Estate Cases in Chapter 11: Are the 1994 Amendments Enough?,* 69 S. CAL. L. REV. 2163, 2184–85 (1996) (noting rising abuse of the current system by single-asset real estate debtors); Brian S. Katz, *Single Asset Real Estate Cases and the Good Faith Requirement: Why Reluctance to Ask Whether a Case Belongs in Bankruptcy May Lead to the Incorrect Result,* 9 BANKR. DEVS. J. 77, 77–78 (1992) (demonstrating the rise of the strategic use of bankruptcy by single-asset real estate debtors); *see also In re* Lumber Exch.

Bldg. Ltd. Partnership, 968 F.2d 647, 650 (8th Cir. 1992) (agreeing with bankruptcy court's conclusion that debtor real estate partnership did not belong in Chapter 11 because it was "substantially a single liability case").

Although some courts concluded that single-asset real estate bankruptcy filings were bad-faith filings subject to dismissal, most courts prior to 1994 concluded that single-asset real estate debtors could file Chapter 11 petitions seeking to reorganize and/or restructure mortgage indebtedness. Erich J. Stegich, *The National Bankruptcy Review Commission: Proposals for Single Asset Real Estate*, 5 AM. BANKR. INST. L. REV. 530 (1997). Nevertheless, Congress perceived that single-asset real estate debtors were abusing the bankruptcy process by filing Chapter 11 petitions to delay mortgage foreclosures even when there was little chance that the debtors could successfully restructure their loans. In response to perceived abuses by real estate debtors, Congress amended the Bankruptcy Code to provide special rules governing single-asset real estate, which the Code defines as

> real property constituting a single property or project, other than residential real property with fewer than 4 residential units, which generates substantially all of the gross income of a debtor and on which no substantial business is being conducted by a debtor other than the business of operating the real property and activities incidental thereto having aggregate noncontingent, liquidated secured debts in an amount no more than $4,000,000 [11 U.S.C. § 101(51B)].

These special rules limit the scope of the automatic stay with regard to single-asset real estate. To ensure the continued protection of the automatic stay, the single-asset real estate debtor must file its reorganization plan within 90 days of the petition date, that plan must have a "reasonable possibility of being confirmed within a reasonable time," and the debtor must begin making monthly payments to the mortgage lender equal to the interest that would accrue at current market rates on the secured portion of the mortgage lender's claim. These rules thus enable the lender holding a mortgage on single-asset real estate significantly more favorable and expedient treatment in bankruptcy than might otherwise result in a traditional Chapter 11 case. For example, in a traditional Chapter 11, the debtor would not be obligated to make interim "adequate protection" payments during the pendency of the bankruptcy unless the mortgaged land was depreciating in value. *See* United Savings Ass'n of Texas v. Timbers of Inwood Forest Assocs., Ltd., 484 U.S. 365 (1988).

Given the quoted definition of "single-asset real estate," a bor-rower's acquisition of other real estate assets or a borrower's expansion of its business beyond the operation of the mortgaged property could de-prive a lender of this more favorable treatment in the event of the bor-rower's bankruptcy. Accordingly, paragraph 22(c) of the Deed of Trust aims to prevent this result by discouraging the borrower from such an acquisition or expansion upon penalty of default. For additional expla-nation, see Section 33.

(d) *fraud or material misrepresentation or material omission by Borrower, or any of its officers, directors, trustees, general partners or managers, Key Principal or any guarantor in connection with (A) the application for or creation of the Indebtedness, (B) any financial statement, rent roll, or other report or information provided to Lender during the term of the Indebtedness, or (C) any request for Lender's consent to any proposed action, including a request for disbursement of funds under any Collateral Agreement;*

Explanation

Fraud or misrepresentation by the borrower. As explained in Section 41, a lender generally decides to fund a mortgage loan based upon the accuracy of certain financial and legal information about the borrower and the mortgaged property. If the lender discovers that this information overstated the borrower's financial strength or the prof-itability of the mortgaged premises in a material fashion, the lender understandably may wish to declare a default and attempt to extract itself from the loan relationship as quickly as possible. Accordingly, paragraph 22(d) of the Deed of Trust authorizes the lender to use ma-terial misstatements or omissions in the borrower's loan application materials as a basis for accelerating the maturity of the mortgage debt.

In addition, lenders generally depend upon obtaining accurate finan-cial and legal information from their borrowers throughout the term of a mortgage loan. This information enables lenders to make prudent judg-ments in monitoring and administering loans, as well as to make informed decisions when borrowers seek consent to take actions otherwise unautho-rized by the mortgage documents. *See supra* Section 14. Accordingly, para-graph 22(d) also authorizes the lender to use material misstatements or omissions in these contexts as a basis for acceleration of the mortgage debt.

(e) *any Event of Default under Section 21;*

Explanation

Due-on-transfer clauses.   In making a mortgage loan, lenders typically make a careful evaluation of the creditworthiness, reputation, and experience of the borrower. Through this evaluation, the lender reaches a conclusion to enter into a significant long-term business relationship with its borrower. Consequently, it is important that while the mortgage debt remains outstanding, the borrower continues to own the mortgaged premises and the identities of those who control the borrower and related entities do not change without the lender's consent. Paragraph 22(e) of the Deed of Trust discourages such unauthorized changes: The lender may treat as an event of default any transfers of the mortgaged premises or any controlling interests in the borrower or related entities in violation of paragraph 21.

Generally speaking, "due-on-sale" or "due-on-transfer" clauses in mortgage documentation are enforceable by virtue of § 341 of the Garn–St. Germain Depository Institutions Act of 1982, 12 U.S.C. § 1701j-3. In some circumstances, courts have struck down as unreasonable restraints on alienation restrictions that were phrased as "promissory restraints," i.e., restrictions that literally prohibited any transfer without the lender's consent (in contrast to a "due-on" clause, whereby the borrower could transfer subject to the risk that the lender might choose to accelerate the maturity of the mortgage debt). *See, e.g.,* North Point Patio Offices Venture v. United Benefit Life Insurance Co., 672 S.W.2d 35 (Tex. Ct. App. 1984). The language of Section 21 of the Deed of Trust, which is a more classic "due-on-transfer" provision, should be freely enforceable in the event of an unconsented-to transfer or change. For further explanation, see Section 21.

(f)   *the commencement of a forfeiture action or proceeding, whether civil or criminal, which, in Lender's reasonable judgment, could result in a forfeiture of the Mortgaged Property or otherwise materially impair the lien created by this Instrument or Lender's interest in the Mortgaged Property;*

Explanation

Forfeiture of the mortgaged property.   Federal and state statutes authorize the forfeiture of property involved in illegal activities such as (among others) gambling, racketeering, money laundering, moonshining, tax evasion, drug trafficking, and pornography. *See, e.g.,* Jimmy Gurulé & Sandra Guerra, The Law of Asset Forfeiture (1998);

David F. B. Smith, *Mortgage Lenders Beware: The Threat to Real Estate Financing Caused by Flawed Protection for Mortgage Lenders in Federal Forfeiture Actions Involving Real Property*, 25 REAL PROP. PROB. & TR. J. 481 (1990). If there is probable cause to believe that a borrower had made use of land in the course of such illegal activities, federal or state governments might institute civil or criminal proceedings to forfeit the borrower's interest in the land. *See, e.g.*, 21 U.S.C. § 881(a)(7) (forfeiture to United States of any right, title, and interest in land used or intended to be used to facilitate commission of drug crimes). If the government prevails, title to the land would vest in the government as of the time of the illegal conduct under the "relation-back" doctrine. *See, e.g.*, United States v. 92 Buena Vista Ave., 507 U.S. 111 (1993). Under the "relation-back" principle, a forfeiture could extinguish the lien of a mortgage granted after the illegal activity took place, unless the forfeiture law permitted the mortgage lender to establish an innocent owner defense. Accordingly, paragraph 22(f) of the Deed of Trust treats as an event of default the institution of any civil or criminal forfeiture proceedings against the mortgaged property. *See also supra* Section 10.

The innocent owner defense.   Most forfeiture statutes provide an innocent owner defense designed to shield the statutes from constitutional challenge. For example, the federal drug forfeiture statute provides that "no property shall be forfeited under this paragraph, to the extent of an interest of an owner, by reason of any act or omission established by that owner to have been committed or omitted without the knowledge or consent of that owner." 21 U.S.C. § 881(a)(7). For many years, governments aggressively pursued forfeiture against such "innocent" owners as spouses, landlords, or lenders based upon the argument that courts should infer "constructive" knowledge of the illegal conduct based upon suspicious circumstances (i.e., they "should have known" about the conduct). Recent decisions, however, have viewed the government's exercise of forfeiture less favorably. For example, in *United States v. One Single Family Residence Located at 6960 Miraflores Ave.*, 995 F.2d 1558 (11th Cir. 1993), the Eleventh Circuit refused to forfeit the mortgage lien of Republic National Bank of Miami ("Republic"). Republic had made an $800,000 bridge loan to a Panamanian corporation, secured by a first mortgage on a home that was to be repaid when the home was sold. A few months later, the United States commenced a civil forfeiture based on its position that the true owner of the land was a reputed drug dealer, Indelcio Iglesias. The government argued that Republic should have known that the corporation was a shell controlled by

Iglesias and that the home was acquired with the proceeds of narcotics trafficking. The Eleventh Circuit held that Republic could avoid forfeiture of its mortgage lien by proof that it lacked actual knowledge of the illegal conduct; further, the court rejected the government's view that actual knowledge could be inferred from some proof of "suspicious circumstances" surrounding the making of the loan.

Although paragraph 22(f) likely is enforceable according to its terms, it is nevertheless of little practical use to the Lender. As drafted, paragraph 22(f) would authorize the lender to declare a default and pursue foreclosure only after the institution of a forfeiture proceeding. Unless the lender can qualify as an "innocent owner" under the provisions of the relevant forfeiture statute, however, most forfeitures (once ordered) will "relate back" to the time the illegal act was committed—thus mooting the lender's belated attempt to exercise its remedies. The lender's only meaningful protection against the risk of forfeiture is careful investigation and monitoring of the activities of its borrowers, in order to maximize its likelihood of establishing the innocent owner defense.

(g)   *any failure by Borrower to perform any of its obligations under this Instrument (other than those specified in Sections 22(a) through (f)), as and when required, which continues for a period of 30 days after notice of such failure by Lender to Borrower, but no such notice or grace period shall apply in the case of any such failure which could, in Lender's judgment, absent immediate exercise by Lender of a right or remedy under this Instrument, result in harm to Lender, impairment of the Note or this Instrument or any other security given under any other Loan Document;*

(h)   *any failure by Borrower to perform any of its obligations as and when required under any Loan Document other than this Instrument which continues beyond the applicable cure period, if any, specified in that Loan Document; and*

Explanation

Nonmonetary defaults.   Mortgage loan documents typically place any number of "nonmonetary" obligations upon a borrower. The Deed of Trust provides several examples of these nonmonetary obligations, such as the obligation to provide annual financial statements during the term of the mortgage loan (*see supra* Section 14, paragraph 14(b)), the obligation to permit no changes in the use of the mortgaged property without the lender's prior consent (*see supra* Section 11), and the obligation to repair and maintain the mortgaged property (*see supra* Section 17, paragraph 17(a)).

Although a lender's primary concern will usually be its borrower's timely payment of its mortgage payments, a borrower's breach of its "nonmonetary" obligations can also pose potentially unacceptable risks to a lender. For example, the borrower's failure to provide current financial statements may compromise the lender's ability to make sound judgments regarding administration and monitoring of the loan. A decision by the borrower to change the use of the premises could threaten the commercial viability of the mortgaged premises (such as a decision by the borrower to convert empty stores in a shopping center to office use, further compromising the marketing of the premises as a shopping center). The borrower's failure to maintain the mortgaged premises in a proper fashion could have an obvious negative effect upon its value, thereby compromising the lender's overall secured position. Paragraphs 22(g) and 22(h) of the Deed of Trust encourage the borrower to perform its nonmonetary obligations in a timely fashion—thereby providing the lender with additional comfort about the current status of the loan—by authorizing the lender to use breach of these nonmonetary obligations as a basis for acceleration of the mortgage loan under paragraph 43.

Notice and opportunity to cure. Mortgage loan documents sometimes require a lender to provide the borrower with notice and a grace period in which to cure any breaches before the lender may use those breaches as a basis for accelerating the maturity of the mortgage debt. Whether the documents include a notice/cure period requirement—and whether any such requirement extends only to nonmonetary defaults or to monetary defaults as well—is typically a function of significant negotiation between borrower and lender. Paragraph 22(g) of the Deed of Trust obligates the lender to provide notice and a 30-day cure period for nonmonetary defaults covered by that section.

Must the lender demonstrate impairment of security to enforce a nonmonetary default? Paragraphs 22(g) and 22(h) purport to authorize the declaration of an event of default following the borrower's failure to cure a nonmonetary default, regardless of the actual threat posed by such failure. Nothing in the Deed of Trust requires the lender to prove that its likelihood of payment or the security of its mortgage lien is impaired or threatened as a result of the borrower's default. Traditionally, most courts have concluded that the mortgagee can place the borrower in default upon the borrower's breach of specific mortgage covenants, even without demonstrating that the lender's security is impaired. Restatement (Third) of Property: Mortgages § 8.1, cmt. a, provides as follows:

[W]here the mortgagee's acceleration stems from the mortgagor's violation of specific covenants, impairment of security need not be shown. Thus, for example, if the mortgage requires the mortgagor to care for an improvement in a certain manner [or] to insure the premises . . ., defaults on these covenants are the proper basis for acceleration even though they . . . do not impair security.

Nevertheless, borrowers faced with acceleration of secured debts have from time to time challenged the right of secured lenders to accelerate the maturity of those debts in the absence of any impairment of security or likelihood of repayment. Many of these challenges are founded upon U.C.C. § 1-203, which imposes a duty of good faith in the performance and enforcement of every contract governed by the U.C.C. (such as a promissory note). Some of these challenges have been successful:

- The Texas Court of Appeals nullified the acceleration of a purchase money mortgage debt and enjoined the foreclosure of that mortgage—even though the mortgagor had failed to pay installments on a timely basis during a title dispute with the seller/mortgagee—on the ground that the circumstances demonstrated no meaningful threat to the mortgagee's security or prospects for repayment. Davis v. Pletcher, 727 S.W.2d 29 (Tex. Civ. App. 1987).

- A Florida bankruptcy court enjoined a national motel franchisor from accelerating a $200 million credit line secured by mortgages on various motel properties—despite the borrower's failure to provide the mortgagee with audited financial statements as required in the loan agreement—because the breach did not impair the mortgagee's security or its prospects for repayment and because acceleration would have placed the borrower in default on more than $220 million of other loans. In re Prime Motor Inns, Inc., 131 B.R. 233 (Bankr. S.D. Fla. 1991).

- Prior to the adoption of the Garn–St. Germain Act, 12 U.S.C. § 1701j-3, which preempted state law restrictions on the use of due-on-sale clauses in most mortgages, a significant number of courts traditionally sustained mortgagor challenges to the exercise of a due-on-sale clause in the absence of any showing by the mortgagee that the sale posed a threat to its security or its likelihood of repayment. See, e.g., Patton v. First Federal Savings & Loan Ass'n, 578 P.2d 152 (Ariz. 1978); Wellenkamp v. Bank of America, 582 P.2d 970 (Cal. 1978); First Federal Savings & Loan Ass'n v. Lockwood,

385 So. 2d 156 (Fla. Dist. Ct. App. 1980); Continental Federal
Savings & Loan Ass'n v. Fetter, 564 P.2d 1013 (Okla. 1977).

Accordingly, could a borrower who failed to provide financial statements to the lender (as required by paragraph 14(b) of the Deed of
Trust) successfully challenge the lender's decision to accelerate the maturity of the mortgage debt based on this failure? A significant number
of courts would reject such a challenge out of hand, based on the view
that the lender cannot be understood to act in "bad faith" if it accelerates a loan based on an express, objective covenant contained in the
loan documentation. One of the best examples is *Kham & Nate's Shoes
No. 2, Inc. v. First Bank of Whiting*, 908 F.2d 1351 (7th Cir. 1990), in
which Judge Easterbrook justified an extremely narrow view of "good
faith" by reference to the need for certainty and predictability in con-
tracting:

> Firms that have negotiated contracts are entitled to enforce them to
> the letter, even to the great discomfort of their trading partners,
> without being mulcted for lack of "good faith." Although courts
> often refer to the obligation of good faith that exists in every con-
> tractual relation, this is not an invitation to the court to decide
> whether one party ought to have exercised privileges expressly re-
> served in the document. "Good faith" is a compact reference to an
> implied undertaking not to take opportunistic advantage in a way
> that could not have been contemplated at the time of drafting, and
> which therefore was not resolved explicitly by the parties. Where
> the contract is silent, principles of good faith—such as the UCC's
> standard of honesty in fact—fill the gap. They do not block use of
> terms that actually appear in the contract.
> . . . [K]nowledge that literal enforcement means some mismatch
> between the parties' expectation and the outcome does not imply a
> general duty of "kindness" in performance, or of judicial oversight
> into whether a party had "good cause" to act as it did. Parties to a
> contract are not each others' fiduciaries; they are not bound to treat
> customers with the same consideration reserved for their families.
> Any attempt to add an overlay of "just cause" . . . to the exercise of
> contractual privileges would reduce commercial certainty and breed
> costly litigation. [908 F.2d at 1357]

Under Judge Easterbrook's view, an accelerating creditor would act in
"good faith" if it honestly believed that the borrower had violated any of
the specific objective covenants in the contract (e.g., by failing to provide
a financial statement or by further encumbering the collateral) and the
contract, on its face, authorized acceleration for that violation.

Judge Easterbrook's view of good faith, however, is more constrained than the view expressed by the Permanent Editorial Board of the Uniform Commercial Code. In PEB Commentary No. 10, the PEB elaborated on the duty of good faith in terms that suggest the need to look beyond the "four corners" of the contract documents:

> The "agreement of the parties" cannot be read off the face of a document, but must be discerned against the background of actual commercial practice. Not only does the Code recognize "the reasonable practices and standards of the commercial community . . . [as] an appropriate source of legal obligation," but it also rejects the "premise that the language used [by the parties] has the meaning attributable to [it] by rules of construction existing in the law rather than the meaning which arises out of the commercial context in which it was used." The correct perspective on the meaning of good faith performance and enforcement is the Agreement of the parties. The critical question is, "Has 'X' acted in good faith with respect to the performance or enforcement of some right or duty under the terms of the Agreement?" *It is therefore wrong to conclude that as long as the agreement allows a party to do something, it is under all terms and conditions permissible.* Such a conclusion overlooks completely the distinction between merely performing or enforcing a right or duty under an agreement on the one hand and, on the other hand, doing so in a way that recognizes that the agreement should be interpreted in a manner consistent with the reasonable expectations of the parties in the light of the commercial conditions existing in the context under scrutiny. The latter is the correct approach. [February 10, 1994 (emphasis added)]

Thus, in the example posed (the lender's acceleration based on the borrower's failure to provide financial statements as required by paragraph 14(b) of the Deed of Trust), PEB Commentary No. 10 suggests that the lender would be acting in good faith in accelerating the debt unless, under the circumstances, acceleration would be inconsistent with the reasonable ex ante expectations of the parties (and would thus constitute an unwarranted or unfair surprise to the borrower). Given that the literal language of the Deed of Trust contemplates acceleration upon the borrower's failure to cure this default, how could such an acceleration be inconsistent with the reasonable ex ante expectations of the parties? As a practical matter, there are a few possibilities that the lender's counsel should appreciate. These may include the following:

- Where the lender's own words or conduct may have led the borrower to believe that its failure would not result in acceleration, courts may well use the doctrines of waiver or estoppel to prevent acceleration of the debt. *See, e.g.,* RESTATEMENT (THIRD) OF PROPERTY: MORTGAGES § 8.1(d).

- If the borrower can demonstrate that the lender has not treated other similarly situated borrowers in similar fashion (e.g., that other borrowers failed to comply with this requirement without having their loans accelerated), the borrower may be able to persuade the court that the lender's decision to accelerate lacks good faith and should not be sustained. In this circumstance, the inconsistency of the lender's actions with its own prior conduct could give rise to an inference that the lender is in fact accelerating the loan for some other (illegitimate) reason and that the stated reason is merely pretextual. Many successful challenges to acceleration involve cases in which the court was suspicious that the stated reason for the lender's acceleration was pretextual. *See, e.g.,* Peoples Bank & Trust Co. v. Cermack, 658 So. 2d 1352 (Miss. 1995) (where secured party waited for two months after debtor further encumbered collateral before accelerating, delay could give rise to the inference that the secured party was accelerating because it deemed itself insecure, and acceleration for insecurity is not permissible unless objectively reasonable); *In re* Martin Specialty Vehicles, 87 B.R. 752 (Bankr. D. Mass. 1988) (secured party wrongfully accelerated installment note for nonpayment of interest when secured party could have covered delinquent installments from funds in debtor's operating account, but instead chose to accelerate to sever ties to borrower after discovering that one of borrower's shareholders was linked to organized crime); Texas Refrigeration Supply, Inc. v. FDIC, 953 F.2d 975 (5th Cir. 1992) (acceleration of maturity of line of credit based upon borrower's failure to provide financial statements unenforceable where record permitted inference that bank's insistence on the financial statement was pretextual).

For further discussion, *see* R. Wilson Freyermuth, *Enforcement of Acceleration Provisions and the Rhetoric of Good Faith,* 1998 BYU L. REV. 1035.

(i) *any exercise by the holder of any other debt instrument secured by a mortgage, deed of trust or deed to secure debt on the Mortgaged Property of a right to declare all amounts due under that debt instrument immediately due and payable.*

Explanation

Default under another mortgage.   If the mortgaged premises are also covered by one or more other mortgages, a decision by another mortgagee to accelerate its mortgage debt could serve as a critical warning flag to the lender. When the party accelerating this other debt is a mortgagee holding a superior mortgage lien, the borrower's default creates the risk of a foreclosure that would extinguish the lender's interest. Such a threat evidently justifies the lender in taking swift action to declare a default and begin exercising its own default remedies.

Even if the other creditor holds a subordinate mortgage, however, such an acceleration provides the lender with a signal that the borrower has defaulted under another mortgage instrument—perhaps calling into serious question either the borrower's financial condition or the ability of the premises to service the mortgage debt in a timely fashion. Thus, paragraph 22(i) of the Deed of Trust authorizes the lender to declare a default when the borrower's default under another mortgage on the mortgaged premises triggers the acceleration of that mortgage debt.

Remedies
Cumulative

Each right and remedy provided in this Instrument is distinct from all other rights or remedies under this Instrument or any other Loan Document or afforded by applicable law, and each shall be cumulative and may be exercised concurrently, independently, or successively, in any order.

Explanation

Lender's choice of remedies.   When a borrower defaults in performing its obligations under the mortgage loan documents, there are numerous remedies potentially available to the lender seeking to be made whole (e.g., to receive payment of the entire amount of debt owed to it under the loan documents and to recover on any indemnities for any additional losses it may have incurred). The most obvious remedy in a mortgage loan situation is to foreclose on the mortgage. If the lender is the successful bidder at the foreclosure sale, the lender will then own the mortgaged property and can resell it to recover the debt owed to it. If another party is the successful bidder, this ordinarily means that this party bid more than the amount of debt owed to the senior mortgage lender, and the senior lender will then be paid off in full.

Sometimes, however, foreclosure of the property will not make the lender whole. If the value of the property is less than the mortgage debt (especially likely if it is a second mortgage loan) or if the

135

mortgage lender is junior in right to other lien holders, the mortgage debt may exceed the proceeds the mortgage lender receives from a foreclosure. In such circumstances, the lender will desire to sue the borrower (if the loan is a recourse loan or if an applicable "carve-out" to nonrecourse liability applies) or any guarantors for the "deficiency" (the difference between the debt owed to the lender and the amount recovered in the foreclosure sale). Furthermore, in some cases, the lender may elect not to foreclose on the mortgage. For example, if there is a serious environmental contamination problem with respect to the mortgaged property, the value of the property will decline. Even if the lender can successfully avoid liability for this contamination under the security interest exemption (*see supra* Section 18), the lender will have difficulty selling the property and recovering its debt. In this circumstance, the lender would prefer to sue the borrower (again if a recourse loan and if the borrower has other assets to recover from) or the guarantors, if any, with respect to the entire amount of the debt.

In addition, sometimes a borrower pledges more than its interest in the real estate project to secure the mortgage loan. For example, the borrower may have delivered a letter of credit to the lender or pledged a certificate of deposit with the lender. The lender will also want to be able to draw on the letter of credit or obtain the funds on deposit to improve its chances of a full recovery. Of course, lenders cannot exercise their rights in a manner that allows them to recover more than the amount of debt owed to them. Lenders might also seek certain remedies during the pendency of the foreclosure action to protect their interest in the mortgaged property, such as seeking the appointment of a receiver or exercising the assignment of rents.

Paragraph 23 of the Deed of Trust attempts to clarify that the lender is entitled to exercise any and all remedies available to it under the law and under the loan documents—either concurrently, independently, or successively, in any order.

Limitations on the lender's choice of remedies.   In jurisdictions that do not limit (or place few limitations upon) the remedies available to lenders after a borrower defaults under a commercial mortgage loan, the clarification on remedies available to the lender as drafted in paragraph 23 should be enforced. *See, e.g.*, Fidelity Mutual Life Insurance Co. v. Chicago Title and Trust Co. of Chicago, 1994 WL 494897 (N.D. Ill. 1994); Ingersoll-Rand Financial Corp. v. Atlantic Management and Consulting Corp., 717 F. Supp. 1067 (D.N.J. 1989).

However, numerous jurisdictions limit the remedies available to a lender after the borrower's default. One key limitation involves the ability of the lender to pursue a deficiency action against the borrower. Some jurisdictions prohibit a deficiency action in certain circumstances, such as when the lender elects to foreclose through the swifter power-of-sale procedure rather than the judicial foreclosure procedure. Some jurisdictions will allow a lender to sue the borrower (for any recourse liability) or any guarantor, but will require that the lender foreclose on the mortgage first. These limitations on remedies are immutable rules or rules of law (e.g., they can not be modified by agreement of the parties at the time that the loan is first made) rather than default rules or rules of construction (which could be modified by agreement of the parties at the time the loan is first made). *See, e.g.,* Jack Erickson & Assocs. v. Hesselgesser, 50 Cal. App. 4th 182, 185, 57 Cal. Rptr. 2d 591, 592 (1996) (purchaser under installment sale cannot waive antideficiency protection in advance, but can waive it by virtue of subsequent conduct); Keever v. Nicholas Beers Co., 96 Nev. 509, 611 P.2d 1079 (1980).

Forbearance

(a) Lender may (but shall not be obligated to) agree with Borrower, from time to time, and without giving notice to, or obtaining the consent of, or having any effect upon the obligations of, any guarantor or other third party obligor, to take any of the following actions: extend the time for payment of all or any part of the Indebtedness; reduce the payments due under this Instrument, the Note, or any other Loan Document; release anyone liable for the payment of any amounts under this Instrument, the Note, or any other Loan Document; accept a renewal of the Note; modify the terms and time of payment of the Indebtedness; join in any extension or subordination agreement; release any Mortgaged Property; take or release other or additional security; modify the rate of interest or period of amortization of the Note or change the amount of the monthly installments payable under the Note; and otherwise modify this Instrument, the Note, or any other Loan Document.

Explanation

The impact of modification agreements. Paragraph 24(a) of the Deed of Trust responds to court decisions that have released guarantors from liability when a lender and borrower have modified the terms of the loan without the guarantor's consent. These decisions have used the reasoning that it is unfair to the guarantor to change the loan in such a manner that it increases the chances that the borrower will default or increases the guarantor's liability under the loan without the guarantor's consent. Once such a modification has occurred without the guarantor's consent, the guarantor is released of all liability under the guaranty. *See, e.g.,* Regency Equities Corp. v. Reiss, 1995 WL 362496 (S.D.N.Y. 1995). Notwithstanding this rationale, some courts will release the guarantor even if the modification is not "material." *See* Crossland Federal Savings Bank v. A. Suna & Co., 935 F. Supp. 184, 199 (E.D.N.Y. 1996). *But see, e.g.,* Friedman v. Millpit Corp., 713 A.2d 1288, 49 Conn. App. 354 (1998) (modification of loan does not discharge the guarantor unless the modification creates a substituted contract or imposes risks on the guarantor fundamentally different from those imposed under the original loan); Levenson v. Haynes, 934 P.2d 300, 123 N.M. 106 (1997) (change in underlying loan that materially modifies legal effect of the loan will discharge the guarantor from the guaranteed obligation, unless the guarantor consents to the change). In light of this risk, lenders attempt to obtain contractual assurance in the loan documents that they in fact have the right to make loan modifications (including releases of persons and collateral) without first notifying and obtaining the guarantor's consent.

When guarantors have signed agreements that waive objections to loan modifications made without notice to them and without their consent, courts have enforced such agreements. *See, e.g.,* Regency Equities Corp. v. Reiss, 1995 WL 362496 (S.D.N.Y. 1995). The reasoning behind this enforcement seems to be that the agreement serves as an advance consent by the guarantor. *See* Crossland Federal Savings Bank v. A. Suna & Co., 935 F. Supp. 184 (E.D.N.Y. 1996). In jurisdictions following the reasoning of these cases, paragraph 24(a) of the Deed of Trust should enable the lender to modify the loan without first notifying and obtaining the guarantor's consent (assuming that similar "waiver/advance consent" language also appears in the guaranty agreement itself).

(b) *Any forbearance by Lender in exercising any right or remedy under the Note, this Instrument, or any other Loan Document or otherwise afforded by applicable law, shall not be a waiver of or preclude the exercise of any other right or remedy. The acceptance by Lender of payment of all or any part of the Indebtedness after the due date of such payment, or in an amount which is less than the required payment, shall not be a waiver of Lender's right to require prompt payment when due of all other payments on account of the Indebtedness or to exercise any remedies for any failure to make prompt payment. Enforcement by Lender of any security for the Indebtedness shall not constitute an election by Lender of remedies so as to preclude the exercise of any other right available to Lender. Lender's receipt of any awards or proceeds under Sections 19 and 20 shall not operate to cure or waive any Event of Default.*

Explanation

Lender's forbearance in exercising remedies. Paragraph 24(b) of the Deed of Trust addresses the situation that exists when the borrower has defaulted under the loan and the lender has failed to insist on strict performance or has failed to exercise its remedies. Paragraph 24(b) attempts to provide that past inaction by the lender does not mean that the lender has waived its remedies or is estopped from insisting on strict performance or exercising remedies for any future defaults. Lenders have included such language in loan documents because many courts have found that when a lender establishes a prior course of dealing in accepting late payments, the lender has waived its ability to declare a default or is estopped from accelerating the debt upon future defaults (at least until the lender makes clear to the borrower that it will in the future insist on strict performance). *See* Greenberg v. Service Business Forms Indus., Inc., 882 F.2d 1538, 1542 (10th Cir. 1989).

There is some case support suggesting that courts will enforce a provision like paragraph 24(b). In *Village of Canon v. Bankers Trust Co.*, 920 F. Supp. 520, 527 (S.D.N.Y. 1996), the loan matured and the borrower continued to make payments to the lender. The borrower alleged that the lender had orally agreed to extend a bridge loan until the borrower found a permanent loan. The lender accepted these payments, but eventually filed a foreclosure action. The borrower alleged, inter alia, that the lender's acceptance of payments after the loan had matured constituted an agreement by the lender to make a new loan and a waiver of any rights the lender had to foreclose the original loan. The loan documents contained provisions for the payment of default interest after default or maturity, election of remedies language, and language providing no waiver of remedies by course of conduct (all similar to the provisions of the Deed of Trust). The court enforced the loan documents as written and rejected the borrower's waiver argument.

When a lender accelerates a debt and seeks foreclosure, however, the lender is subject to equitable principles. Under the circumstances of a specific case, if a court finds that the lender has acted inequitably, the court may not permit the acceleration and foreclosure, notwithstanding language to the contrary in the loan documents. For example, if a lender had allowed a borrower to pay monthly interest 10 days late for over two years, and then suddenly institutes a foreclosure action in year 3 when the borrower again pays 10 days late, a court would likely find that the lender had waived the right to insist upon timely payment or was estopped from suddenly insisting on strict performance, notwithstanding language such as that contained in paragraph 24(b). *See* Penn Mutual Life Ins. Co. v. Bank of New England Corp., 756 F. Supp. 856, 858 (E.D. Pa. 1991). *See also supra* Section 22, paragraph 22(a).

Loan Charges

If any applicable law limiting the amount of interest or other charges permitted to be collected from Borrower is interpreted so that any charge provided for
in any Loan Document, whether considered separately or together with other
charges levied in connection with any other Loan Document, violates that law,
and Borrower is entitled to the benefit of that law, that charge is hereby reduced to the extent necessary to eliminate that violation. The amounts, if any,
previously paid to Lender in excess of the permitted amounts shall be applied
by Lender to reduce the principal of the Indebtedness. For the purpose of determining whether any applicable law limiting the amount of interest or other
charges permitted to be collected from Borrower has been violated, all
Indebtedness which constitutes interest, as well as all other charges levied in
connection with the Indebtedness which constitute interest, shall be deemed to
be allocated and spread over the stated term of the Note. Unless otherwise required by applicable law, such allocation and spreading shall be effected in
such a manner that the rate of interest so computed is uniform throughout the
stated term of the Note.

Explanation

Limits on interest and other charges. Paragraph 25 of the Deed of
Trust mainly addresses the issue of usurious interest charges. Paragraph
25 provides a general "savings" clause: To the extent that the amount of

any interest or other charges under the loan might violate any law as being excessive, the amount is reduced to the extent necessary to eliminate a violation. Further, paragraph 25 also provides specific methods to avoid a violation of law (e.g., spreading the amount paid over the term of the loan or applying it to the principal portion of the debt).

In addition to interest, other loan charges (such as late fees and default interest) are susceptible to challenge, but results have been mixed. *See* Metlife Capital Financial Corp. v. Washington Ave. Assocs., L.P., 313 N.J. Super. 525, 713 A.2d 527 (1998) (in commercial mortgage loan, court held that 5 percent late fee and default rate of interest equal to stated rate plus 3 percent constituted unenforceable penalties, because they were not related to any damages the lender suffered in connection with the borrower's defaults in making payments), *rev'd*, Metlife Capital Financial Corp. v. Washington Ave. Assocs., L.P., 732 A.2d 493 (N.J. 1999) (concluding that 3 percent incremental default rate was "a reasonable estimate of potential damages" and fell "well within the range demonstrated to be customary"; default interest provision is "stipulated damages clause negotiated between sophisticated commercial entities" and should be treated as presumptively reasonable). *See also infra* Section 43.

Some courts have enforced savings clauses such as those appearing in paragraph 25. *See, e.g., In re* Wright, 144 B.R. 943 (Bankr. S.D. Ga. 1992) (loan fee spread over life of loan, not applied exclusively to first month of loan); *and* Pentico v. Mad-Wayler, Inc., 964 S.W.2d 708 (Tex. App. 1998) (interest spread over term of loan to avoid usury). However, some courts will not enforce this type of savings clause. *See, e.g.,* Swindell v. Federal Nat'l Mortgage Ass'n, 409 S.E.2d 892 (N.C. 1991) (usury savings clause in mortgage note could not shield mortgagee from liability for charging usurious late payment fee). In *Swindell*, the court noted that there were two purposes behind late payment fees: to encourage the borrower to pay on time and to compensate the lender for the period of the delay. The court ruled that in light of this second purpose, the 5 percent charge imposed for payments made more than fifteen 15 days late was "interest" within the meaning of the North Carolina statute (*id.* at 894), and that the rate charged exceeded the maximum rate permitted under the usury statute (*id.* at 895). The court held that the usury savings clause in the note could not shield the lender from liability for charging usurious rates because such a holding would be inconsistent with the policies behind the usury statute (to protect borrowers by putting the burden of compliance on the lender). If the usury savings clause were valid, the court asserted, this would shift the onus back to the borrower to determine that the contract rate was invalid when the burden should be on the lender. The court invalidated only the late charge amount, not all interest due on the note. *Id.* at 896.

Although the *Swindell* case appears at first blush unfavorable to lenders, some of its dicta could in fact be useful to lenders. As noted, the court in *Swindell* stated that there were two purposes to a late charge, one of which was to encourage the borrower to pay on time. If this is a legitimate purpose, then lenders can argue that the charge should not be invalidated as an invalid liquidated damages penalty (unless the amount is unconscionable). *See* Dacon Bolingbrook Assocs. Ltd. Partnership. v. Federal Nat'l Mortgage Ass'n, 155 B.R. 467 (N.D. Ill. 1993) (enforcing 4 percent late charge and stating that valid purpose of late charges is to encourage borrower's timely payment); Travelers Ins. Co. v. Corporex Properties, Inc., 798 F. Supp. 423 (E.D. Ky. 1992) (court enforced 4 percent late charge as reasonable).

Due to the strong public policies behind usury laws and the different approaches jurisdictions take to this issue, it is dangerous to generalize on the enforceability of paragraph 25 of the Deed of Trust. One must look to the laws of the jurisdiction whose law controls with respect to any specific loan transaction on any issue—especially this issue.

Waiver of Statute of Limitations

Borrower hereby waives the right to assert any statute of limitations as a bar to the enforcement of the lien of this Instrument or to any action brought to enforce any Loan Document.

Explanation

Can the borrower waive the statute of limitations? The primary causes of action that a lender might seek against a borrower under a mortgage loan are for a judgment for the debt due, for foreclosure of the mortgage, for a deficiency judgment against the borrower, or for a judgment against a guarantor. One would expect a lender to proceed with any of these actions promptly, and thus would not expect the statute of limitations to arise in enforcement actions. In Illinois, for example, a lender can bring an action to foreclose on the mortgage so long as the lender does so within 10 years after the right of action accrues. 735 ILL. COMP. STAT. 5/13-115. Indeed, in some jurisdictions there is no statute of limitations applicable to an in rem foreclosure proceeding, but only to an action on the contract for a monetary judgment. *See, e.g.,* United States v. Begin, 160 F. 3d 1319 (Cal. 1998) (six-year period applicable to judgment on note, but not to in rem foreclosure proceedings); *but see* Draggs v. Ewell, 6 F. Cas. 1109 (Cir. Ct. W.D. Tex. 1879) (if debt barred by statute of limitations, foreclosure suit is barred as well, as mortgage is mere incident of debt), *aff'd,* 108 U.S. 143 (1883).

However, special circumstances can bring the statute of limitations into issue. For example, a lender may wish to sue under an environmental indemnity agreement, but not until some date well after an environmental issue arises. Likewise, loan workouts can sometimes drag on for years, and it may be possible that a given jurisdiction's statute of limitations could be raised as a bar to a suit. In addition, if the mortgage does not adequately state when the loan matures, in some jurisdictions the statute of limitations begins to run on the date the mortgage is executed. *See* McCray v. Twitchell, 112 Idaho 787, 789, 735 P.2d 1098, 1100 (Idaho Ct. App. 1987).

Some courts have enforced a written waiver of the statute of limitations in the context of a suit to foreclose a lien. *See* United States v. American Gas Screw Franz Joseph, 210 F. Supp. 581, 583 (D. Alaska 1962). Indeed, one court has held that the borrower's waiver of the right to raise the statute of limitations is also enforceable against a junior lender. Kaichen's Metal Mar, Inc. v. Ferro Cast Co., 33 Cal. App. 4th 8 (1995).

Consequently, paragraph 26 of the Deed of Trust could prove useful to a lender in exceptional circumstances. Even in jurisdictions that recognize this waiver (or do not contain a statute of limitations for a foreclosure action, but instead a presumption of satisfaction 20 years after maturity), however, it may still be possible for a borrower to estop the lender from foreclosing on the basis of equitable principles and the doctrine of laches. *See* B.E. Williamson v. Shoults, 423 So. 2d 874, 876 (Ala. App. 1982).

Waiver of Marshaling

Notwithstanding the existence of any other security interests in the Mortgaged Property held by Lender or by any other party, Lender shall have the right to determine the order in which any or all of the Mortgaged Property shall be subjected to the remedies provided in this Instrument, the Note, any other Loan Document or applicable law. Lender shall have the right to determine the order in which any or all portions of the Indebtedness are satisfied from the proceeds realized upon the exercise of such remedies. Borrower and any party who now or in the future acquires a security interest in the Mortgaged Property and who has actual or constructive notice of this Instrument waives any and all right to require the marshaling of assets or to require that any of the Mortgaged Property be sold in the inverse order of alienation or that any of the Mortgaged Property be sold in parcels or as an entirety in connection with the exercise of any of the remedies permitted by applicable law or provided in this Instrument.

Explanation

Marshaling. Marshaling is a doctrine that determines the order of foreclosure when a mortgage covers multiple parcels. For example, if two parcels are covered by the mortgage, and one of them has a junior lien on it while the other does not, marshaling would dictate that the lender first foreclose upon the parcel without the junior lien. The reason is that this parcel might bring a sufficient price in foreclosure to pay

the debt in full, so that a foreclosure of the other parcel would be un-
necessary. The basic purpose of marshaling, then, is to avoid unneces-
sary harm to the holders of junior interests in the mortgaged property.
See RESTATEMENT (THIRD) OF PROPERTY: MORTGAGES § 8.6 (1997); G.
NELSON & D. WHITMAN, REAL ESTATE FINANCE LAW §§ 10.9–10.15 (3d
ed. 1993).

If the Deed of Trust covers only a single parcel, marshaling might be
considered irrelevant. (Note, however, that marshaling might still apply,
at least in theory, because the Deed of Trust also contains a personal
property security agreement—which employs "other property" besides
the real estate as collateral.) If the mortgage covers more than one real
estate parcel, marshaling is quite likely to be an issue.

In general, senior lenders do not like marshaling. In theory, marshaling does not prejudice their interests; they can still have resort, eventually,
to all of their security if need be. However, marshaling tends to slow down
the foreclosure process and to require more of the lender's time and attention. Understandably, senior lenders prefer to avoid it.

Can the senior mortgagee limit a junior mortgagee's right to marshal?
There is no real doubt that the right to marshal can be waived by language
in the *junior* mortgage—a mortgage held by a lender with a right to request
marshaling. *See, e.g.,* Raynor v. Raynor, 193 S.E.2d 216 (N.C. 1937). The
question raised by paragraph 27 of the Deed of Trust is whether language in
the *senior* mortgage can deprive a *junior* lienholder of the right to request
marshaling. This question is largely unanswered in the case law. The argument that it can do so is based on the principle of notice: If the senior mortgage (with its "waiver of marshaling" clause) is recorded, any persons taking
junior liens on the property are on constructive notice of that clause, and
hence of the fact that they will not be able to assert marshaling. Under this
logic, there is no unfairness to them in denying marshaling; if they considered the loss of the right to marshal to be unacceptable, one might argue,
they should not have made junior loans on this property!

Comments in the Restatement take the position that this sort of "advance waiver" of the right to marshal is valid and enforceable. RESTATEMENT
(THIRD) OF PROPERTY: MORTGAGES § 8.6 cmt. e. *Accord* Platte Valley Bank
v. Kracl, 174 N.W.2d 724 (Neb. 1970); Thompson v. Thomas, 195 P. 427
(Cal. App. 1919). Whether other courts will follow this authority is by no
means certain. Marshaling is an equitable doctrine, and a court of equity, in
a foreclosure proceeding, might apply it despite the fact that the junior
lienor had notice of the waiver clause in the senior mortgage.

Further Assurances

Borrower shall execute, acknowledge, and deliver, at its sole cost and expense, all further acts, deeds, conveyances, assignments, estoppel certificates, financing statements, transfers and assurances as Lender may require from time to time in order to better assure, grant, and convey to Lender the rights intended to be granted, now or in the future, to Lender under this Instrument and the Loan Documents.

Explanation

Further assurances as a title covenant.   Paragraph 28 of the Deed of Trust serves two distinct functions. First, it constitutes, on behalf of the borrower, a covenant for title analogous to the "covenant of further assurances" traditionally recognized by the common law as one of the six covenants for title provided in a general warranty deed. (The title warranties contained in the unnumbered introductory paragraphs of the Deed of Trust do not expressly state such a covenant.) The common-law covenant of further assurances obligates the grantor to execute or cause to be executed, upon the grantee's request, any additional documents necessary to perfect the title that the grantor's original deed purported to convey to the grantee. WILLIAM B. STOEBUCK & DALE A. WHITMAN, THE LAW OF PROPERTY § 11.13, at 910 (3d ed. 2000). Accordingly, paragraph 28 would obligate the borrower to execute any document necessary to cure any curable defect in the borrower's title to the mortgaged premises (excepting, of course, those defects "listed in a schedule of exceptions to coverage in any title insurance policy issued to Lender contemporaneously with" the execution of the Deed of Trust). If the borrower refused to execute such a document, the lender could obtain specific performance to compel the borrower's performance of the covenant. *See, e.g.,* Spiegel v. Seaman, 390 A.2d 639 (N.J. Super. 1978). Because after-acquired title generally inures to the benefit of the grantee without a further conveyance under the doctrine of estoppel by deed, however, the lender would rarely need to assert paragraph 28 for title purposes.

Further assurances and the duty of good faith.   Second, paragraph 28 serves as the borrower's covenant to perform any and all acts as the lender requires in order to provide the lender with assurance of the rights intended to be granted to it under the Deed of Trust and related loan documents. This covenant goes beyond matters of title. Furthermore, because paragraph 22(g) (*see supra* Section 22) would render the borrower's noncompliance with this covenant an event of default if not cured in a timely fashion following notice, paragraph 28 raises some question about its scope.

Few courts have interpreted "further assurances" clauses in this context. In one recent decision, *Madera Production Co. v. Atlantic Richfield Co.*, 1998 WL 292872 (1998), the U.S. District Court for the Northern District of Texas held that a further assurances clause obligates the responsible party to do whatever is necessary to fulfill the purposes of a contract and thus is coextensive with the duty of good faith implied in every contract. Thus, the *Madera* court concluded that "how [a jurisdiction's] courts interpret the obligation to behave in good faith may suggest how a court should interpret the language contained in [a] further assurances clause." Under this view, the lender could not use paragraph 28 as a basis for insisting upon assurances that were outside the scope of the parties' ex ante bargain and would thus come as an unwarranted or unfair surprise to the borrower. As a result, the lender likely could not use paragraph 28 to require the borrower to execute documents that were not expressly or impliedly covered by other substantive provisions of the loan documents.

An example of this view can be seen in another recent decision, *Deville Court Apts., L.P. v. Federal Home Loan Mortgage Corp.*, 39 F. Supp. 2d 428 (D. Del. 1999), which provides an example of how a mortgagee's reliance on a future assurances clause may be unavailing. In this case, Deville (owner of a New Castle County apartment complex encumbered by a $3.675 million mortgage note held by Freddie Mac) entered into a loan modification agreement with Freddie Mac allowing it to refinance the existing loan for a reduced amount if Deville satisfied certain conditions— one of which required the refinanced loan to be with recourse against the general partners. Deville obtained a loan commitment from PNC Bank that provided that the loan would subsequently be transferred on a nonrecourse basis, and accordingly Freddie Mac rejected the commitment. Deville then obtained another commitment omitting any reference to a subsequent transfer. Counsel for Freddie Mac, concerned about the possibility of a side agreement between Deville and PNC Bank to eliminate the personal guarantees of the general partners, requested further assurances as to the terms of the new commitment. These assurances included

- Sworn affidavits from the general partners that the loan documents executed by the general partners in conjunction with the refinancing "are all of the documents evidencing [the loan] and any agreement to transfer such [loan] to . . . any other lender."

- A legal opinion from the borrower's counsel, in a form acceptable to Freddie Mac, that the general partners would be unconditionally personally liable for the refinanced loan amount and "that there are no commitments, understandings, or agreements in writing or otherwise that [the loan] is to become non-recourse upon the transfer of [the loan] or some other event."

When Deville refused, PNC Bank terminated the loan commitment and Deville sued Freddie Mac for breach of the loan modification agreement.

Denying Freddie Mac's motion for summary judgment, the district court concluded that its conditions for the refinancing were unreasonable. Because PNC Bank could have entered into an agreement with another bank to transfer the loan, unbeknownst to the general partners, the court held that Freddie Mac could not reasonably expect the general partners to sign an affidavit that there were no other documents evidencing any agreement to transfer the loan, nor could it reasonably expect Deville's counsel to opine that there were no such agreements. *Id.* at 432. (The court did suggest that Freddie Mac's requirements might have been reasonable if the assurances had been limited to the personal knowledge of Deville's general partners and legal counsel.)

Estoppel Certificate

Within 10 days after a request from Lender, Borrower shall deliver to Lender a written statement, signed and acknowledged by Borrower, certifying to Lender or any person designated by Lender, as of the date of such statement, (i) that the Loan Documents are unmodified and in full force and effect (or, if there have been modifications, that the Loan Documents are in full force and effect as modified and setting forth such modifications); (ii) the unpaid principal balance of the Note; (iii) the date to which interest under the Note has been paid; (iv) that Borrower is not in default in paying the Indebtedness or in performing or observing any of the covenants or agreements contained in this Instrument or any of the other Loan Documents (or, if the Borrower is in default, describing such default in reasonable detail); (v) whether or not there are then existing any setoffs or defenses known to Borrower against the enforcement of any right or remedy of Lender under the Loan Documents; and (vi) any additional facts requested by Lender.

Explanation

Facilitating secondary market sales. Paragraph 29 of the Deed of Trust facilitates a secondary market sale or pledge of the mortgage loan by the lender. Any party who might purchase the loan or accept it as collateral for repayment of some other advance of credit is naturally concerned about the loan's status and whether the borrower has any defenses to payment.

The estoppel certificate described in paragraph 29 is designed to allay those concerns.

Holder-in-due-course status.   When a secondary market sale or pledge of a mortgage loan occurs, the promissory note is the main representation of the loan asset, and the mortgage is simply an adjunct to the note. Traditionally, transferees of notes have relied on the holder-in-due-course doctrine, embodied in U.C.C. Article 3, to protect them from at least some defenses that the maker of the note might attempt to raise. However, holder-in-due-course status is available to the transferee of the note only if the note itself is negotiable in form. See U.C.C. § 3-104 *et seq.* Whether the note that typically accompanies the Deed of Trust is negotiable is a debatable point. Even if it is, however, the holder-in-due-course doctrine protects the transferee of the note only from so-called "personal" defenses—not from "real" defenses, such as infancy, duress, lack of capacity, illegality, fraud in the execution, and discharge in insolvency. See U.C.C. § 3-305(a)(1); Bankers Trust (Delaware) v. 236 Beltway Investment, 865 F. Supp. 1186 (E.D. Va. 1994). Thus, the holder-in-due-course doctrine provides only limited protection for secondary-market transferees of mortgage notes.

Estoppel certificates compared.   An estoppel certificate can offer much stronger protection than holder-in-due-course status. An estoppel certificate is effective whether the promissory note is negotiable or not, and it can exclude *all* defenses of the maker, not merely the "personal" defenses. The estoppel certificate's primary purpose is not to act as a release of any defenses the maker of the note might raise, but simply to get those defenses out "on the table" so that the secondary-market investor can examine them and determine whether they are serious enough to cause the investor to decide not to complete the purchase or loan. The matters that can be discovered in this way are sometimes called "patent equities," because they can be brought to light by means of an estoppel certificate. The certificate should recite that it will be relied upon by persons who are acquiring or lending on the security of the mortgage note.

In addition to bringing any defenses of the maker to light, the estoppel certificate is also useful to a secondary-market investor in verifying the lender's representations concerning the loan's documentation, the current principal and interest outstanding, and the absence of any default. Paragraph 29 permits the lender to ask for "any additional facts" that the lender deems significant. For example, if the note bears an adjustable interest rate, the investor may want confirmation of the current rate. The investor may also wish to confirm, through the estoppel certificate, the balance in any escrow or reserve accounts, the status of insurance coverage on the property, and the existence and unencumbered status of items of personal property. Finally, the investor may wish to confirm that the borrower still owns the real estate and associated personal property, and has not made any transfers in violation of the due-on-sale clause.

The protection that an estoppel certificate offers to secondary-market investors against the note maker's defenses is not perfect. For example, the maker of the note might later claim that even the estoppel statement was induced by fraud, that he or she signed it under duress or undue influence. Such a claim was sustained in *Hammelburger v. Foursome Inn Corp.*, 54 N.Y.2d 580, 431 N.E.2d 278 (1981). Moreover, it is possible that the maker might freely sign a "clean" estoppel statement and only subsequently discover that he or she had a defense; *see, e.g.*, Hendrickson v. Alpert, 412 P.2d 433 (Colo. 1966) (maker did not discover that he had been defrauded until after note and deed of trust were transferred). Obviously, the maker cannot estop himself against a defense he did not know he had. Despite these limitations, estoppel certificates are immensely useful to parties who buy or lend on the security of mortgage notes.

Governing Law; Consent to Jurisdiction and Venue

section 30

(a) *This Instrument, and any Loan Document which does not itself expressly identify the law that is to apply to it, shall be governed by the laws of the jurisdiction in which the Land is located (the **"Property Jurisdiction"**).*

Explanation

Choice of law.   Paragraph 30(a) provides that the terms of the Deed of Trust and the note it secures will be governed by the laws of the state in which the mortgaged property is located (the "forum state"). This choice-of-law provision conforms to the general approach taken by courts with respect to the construction, validity, and effect of the mortgage. The express statement contained in paragraph 30(a) can prove helpful, particularly when the mortgage loan is negotiated, executed, or performed in one jurisdiction and/or one or more of the parties to the transaction reside in a different jurisdiction.

Sometimes—particularly with a loan secured by real property in multiple states—the loan documents contain a choice-of-law provision that selects a state other than the applicable forum state. In a multistate secured loan, lenders sometimes choose the laws of a jurisdiction that they are more familiar with. In addition, lenders sometimes hope to avoid problematic laws of a given jurisdiction (such as antideficiency laws or usury limitations) by providing for the choice of a more favorable jurisdiction's laws.

159

Paragraph 30(a)'s choice-of-law provision is clearly enforceable. The validity of a real estate mortgage and its construction, and the capacity of the parties to the mortgage and their rights under it are all governed by the laws of the forum state, even when the mortgage is executed in another state and the parties reside in another state. *See, e.g.,* Connor v. Elliot, 79 Fla. 524, 85 So. 164 (1920); Guardian Life Ins. Co. of America v. Rita Realty Co., 5 A.2d 45 (N.J. Super. 1939).

To what extent, then, will courts enforce an expressed intent for another jurisdiction's laws to govern the mortgage loan? There are exceptions to the general principle that the laws of the forum state will govern a real estate loan. The parties to a mortgage loan may select a different jurisdiction's laws with respect to actions that do not directly affect title to real property (matters that do directly affect title include the validity of conveyances, warranties, and foreclosures). *Guardian,* 5 A.2d at 49. It is interesting to note that one court, in dicta, stated that antideficiency laws are examples of actions that do not directly affect title to real property. First Commerce Realty Investors v. K-F Land Co., 617 S.W.2d 806, 809 (Tex. App. 1981). This does not necessarily mean, however, that one can avoid antideficiency laws that exist in the jurisdiction where the mortgaged property is located. For the choice of law to be enforced, it must be shown that the parties acted in good faith (not with the purpose of evading the laws of the state where the property is located) and that the provision at issue does not violate the public policy of the state where the property is located. Ferdie Sievers & Lake Tahoe Land Co. v. Diversified Mortgage Investors, 603 P.2d 270, 271 (Nev. 1979). Thus, for example, if the parties have stipulated a fair and reasonable rate of interest valid under laws of a state to which the transaction has a substantial nexus and there is not a clear effort to avoid the laws of the forum state, the provision should not be found to violate the public policy of the forum state. If, in contrast, the interest rate is substantially above what the forum state would allow, so as to shock the conscience of the court, then the court may not honor the choice of law.

Selecting the law of the forum state to govern the transaction usually makes sense and will be enforceable. Sometimes, as with multistate loans, it may make sense to select the laws of another jurisdiction with respect to matters that do not directly affect title. If the provision at issue does not directly affect title matters, it is possible that a court will honor the choice of a different jurisdiction's laws if the provision does not contravene fundamental policy of the forum state, and the chosen state bears at least a reasonable relationship to the parties and the transaction. *See, e.g.,* Hengel, Inc. v. Hot'N Now, Inc., 825 F. Supp. 1311 (N.D. Ill. 1993).

The selection of the choice of law and its enforcement can be a complicated matter. Consequently, if one is involved in a multistate collateral loan, it would be prudent to become familiar with the laws of each state where the collateral is located and to take efforts to comply with such laws.

(b) *Borrower agrees that any controversy arising under or in relation to the Note, this Instrument, or any other Loan Document shall be litigated exclusively in the Property Jurisdiction. The state and federal courts and authorities with jurisdiction in the Property Jurisdiction shall have exclusive jurisdiction over all controversies which shall arise under or in relation to the Note, any security for the Indebtedness, or any other Loan Document. Borrower irrevocably consents to service, jurisdiction, and venue of such courts for any such litigation and waives any other venue to which it might be entitled by virtue of domicile, habitual residence or otherwise.*

Explanation

Jurisdiction and venue. Paragraph 30(b) of the Deed of Trust provides for the borrower's consent to service of process, jurisdiction, and venue of the courts (state and federal) in the jurisdiction where the mortgaged property is located and the waiver of claims to the contrary based upon the borrower's domicile or residence elsewhere. As discussed above, the choice of the law and the courts of the forum state usually makes sense in the typical case, but may not make sense in a multistate mortgage loan. Although the laws of the respective forum states may govern certain matters, it may be best to litigate as many of the other issues as possible in a single jurisdiction. To increase the chances of this result, paragraph 30(b) provides for consent to service of process, jurisdiction, and venue, including waiver of a claim to a different venue that may have connections to the loan transaction or the parties.

There is authority for enforcement of a contractual waiver of an objection to venue. In *First Nat'l Bank of Eastern Arkansas v. Arkansas Dev. Fin. Auth.*, 870 S.W.2d 400 (Ark. App. 1994), the court enforced the venue specified in the agreement between the parties even though this agreement was for a venue different from what a statute would have provided. 870 S.W.2d at 403.

Notice

(a) *All notices, demands and other communications ("notice") under or concerning this Instrument shall be in writing. Each notice shall be addressed to the intended recipient at its address set forth in this Instrument, and shall be deemed given on the earliest to occur of (1) the date when the notice is received by the addressee; (2) the first Business Day after the notice is delivered to a recognized overnight courier service, with arrangements made for payment of charges for next Business Day delivery; or (3) the third Business Day after the notice is deposited in the United States mail with postage prepaid, certified mail, return receipt requested. As used in this Section 31, the term "Business Day" means any day other than a Saturday, a Sunday or any other day on which Lender is not open for business.*

Explanation

Notice. Effective monitoring of the mortgage loan requires effective communication between the borrower and lender regarding the status of the loan. Numerous provisions of the Deed of Trust obligate the parties to provide notice of information or events relevant to the status of the loan. Paragraph 31(a) clarifies issues regarding both the form and timing of such notices.

163

Must the notice be in writing?   Paragraph 31(a) makes clear that any notice required under the loan documents must be in writing. This approach avoids the evidentiary and related problems associated with attempts by one party to provide notice orally (either in person or by telephone). For example, § 9-504(3) of the 1972 text of the Uniform Commercial Code did not specify that notification to the debtor prior to the sale of personal property collateral had to be in writing. A significant body of litigation developed addressing whether oral notification was sufficient to satisfy Article 9's requirement for a commercially reasonable disposition; *compare*, *e.g.*, *In re* Excello Press, Inc., 890 F.2d 896 (7th Cir. 1989) (approving oral notification) *with* Van Ness v. First State Bank of Ida Grove, 430 N.W.2d 109 (Iowa 1988) (writing required). As a result, revised Article 9 requires any presale notification to appear in writing (or in an authenticated record, thereby including information stored in electronic form and capable of being retrieved in perceivable form). U.C.C. § 9-611(c) (1999).

Must the borrower actually receive the notice?   Where the obligation to provide notice arises, the provisions of the Deed of Trust generally refer only to "giving" notice or "delivering" notice; they do not specify that the intended recipient must actually receive the notice. *See, e.g.*, paragraph 18(f) (obligation to notify lender regarding environmental matters) and paragraph 19(b) (obligation to deliver original or duplicate renewal insurance policy). Paragraph 31(a) provides that as long as the notice is directed to the recipient's address as specified in the Deed of Trust, any such notice is deemed given on the first business day after it is deposited for next-business-day delivery with a recognized overnight courier (such as Federal Express) or on the third business day after it is deposited into the United States mail (certified mail, return receipt requested). Under this provision, for example, suppose that the borrower fails to provide financial statements as required by paragraph 14. Under paragraph 22(g), the lender must provide notice of this failure to the borrower (with the borrower having 30 days to cure the failure) before the lender can declare an event of default. Under paragraph 31(a), if the lender deposits written notice of the borrower's failure to provide the financial statements into the U.S. mail on Monday, June 1, via postage-prepaid certified mail, return receipt requested, the lender will be deemed to have given notice on Thursday, June 4—thereby triggering the borrower's 30-day grace period—even if the borrower does not actually receive the notice.

Must the lender attempt to ascertain the borrower's new location?
Suppose that the lender becomes aware that the borrower's address has changed, although the borrower has not effectively changed its address

for notices under paragraph 31(b). Can the lender provide notice at the old address—knowing it is no longer correct—and nevertheless still obtain the benefit of paragraph 31(a)'s "deemed given" provision?

Case law under U.C.C. Article 9—which comparably provides that notice is effective when "sent" rather than when received—is instructive. If an Article 9 secured party knows that the debtor has moved and is aware of the new address, several courts have held that the secured party cannot rely on the old address and must send a notice to the new address. *See, e.g., In re Carter,* 511 F.2d 1203 (9th Cir. 1975). If the secured party knows the debtor has moved but does not have the new address (as it might know if previous notices had been returned "undeliverable—no forwarding address"), some courts have even imposed upon the secured party a duty to take minimal steps to locate and notify the debtor. *See, e.g., Mallicoat v. Volunteer Fin. & Loan Co.,* 415 S.W.2d 347 (Tenn. App. 1966). The comments to revised Article 9 suggest that a secured party who sends a notification and later learns that the debtor did not receive it may have to attempt to locate the debtor and send another notice. *See* U.C.C. § 9-611, cmt. 6 (1999) (leaving to "judicial resolution" whether requirement of reasonable notification requires "second try" by secured party). Thus, even though paragraph 31(a) specifies that notice is "deemed given" if sent to the borrower at the original stated address, the lender who is aware that the borrower's address has changed should not rely on that provision unless the borrower's new address simply cannot be located.

(b) *Any party to this Instrument may change the address to which notices intended for it are to be directed by means of notice given to the other party in accordance with this Section 31. Each party agrees that it will not refuse or reject delivery of any notice given in accordance with this Section 31, that it will acknowledge, in writing, the receipt of any notice upon request by the other party and that any notice rejected or refused by it shall be deemed for purposes of Section 31 to have been received by the rejecting party on the date so refused or rejected, as conclusively established by the records of the U.S. Postal Service or the courier service.*

Explanation

Change of address for notice. Paragraph 31(b) of the Deed of Trust provides a convenient mechanism for the parties to change the address for relevant notices in the event one of the parties relocates.

Often, a borrower in financial distress may attempt to delay the lender in its enforcement of the loan by refusing notices or other demands and thereafter attempting to argue that necessary notices or demands were not provided. Paragraph 31(b) provides a stipulation that refused or rejected notices shall be deemed to have been received on the date refused or rejected, as "conclusively" established by the records of the postal service or courier. To the extent that the address to which the notice is sent remains the correct address, of course, the borrower's rejection or refusal to accept the notice should be irrelevant under paragraph 31(a), which does not require receipt of the notice.

(c)   *Any notice under the Note and any other Loan Document which does not specify how notices are to be given shall be given in accordance with this Section 31.*

Explanation

Notices required by other loan documents.   Paragraph 31(c) of the Deed of Trust is of only minor importance, although it may prove useful if one party needs to provide notification pursuant to a collateral loan document that itself does not provide a notification provision. To the extent that the promissory note and/or other collateral loan documents do provide their own notification provisions, the lender should ensure that the provisions are essentially identical in substance to paragraph 31. This should minimize or eliminate the risk that the lender might give any required notice in a fashion that fails to satisfy the lender's notification obligations.

Sale of Note; Change in Servicer

The Note or a partial interest in the Note (together with this Instrument and the other Loan Documents) may be sold one or more times without prior notice to Borrower. A sale may result in a change of the Loan Servicer. There also may be one or more changes of the Loan Servicer unrelated to a sale of the Note. If there is a change of the Loan Servicer, Borrower will be given notice of the change.

Explanation

Mortgage servicing. Most large mortgage loans on income-producing property are held by institutional lenders (e.g., life insurance companies and pension funds) or by REMIC trustees of securitized mortgage pools. In both cases, the holder of the loan usually does not have the facilities and expertise to service the loan, and hence employs a separate entity to perform the servicing, including collection and remittance of loan payments and maintenance of various reserve accounts. *See infra* Section 39. For example, a trustee of a securitized pool may use both a "master servicer" who performs routine collections and a "special servicer" who takes over the servicing function (including foreclosure and negotiation of workout agreements) for any loans that enter default status.

Paragraph 32 of the Deed of Trust simply warns the borrower that a secondary-market transfer of the property may occur, and that (with or without a secondary-market transfer) a change of servicer may also occur. There is no legal requirement that a borrower be given notice in the mortgage documents that this may happen. By way of comparison, the Real Estate Settlement Procedures Act (RESPA) requires extensive disclosures concerning servicing transfers, but these apply only to one-to-four-family residential "federally related" loans. *See* 12 U.S.C. § 2605 (providing for disclosure at time of loan application of percentage of lender's loans that have experienced transfer of servicing during previous three years, and for notice of any actual transfer of servicing); Robert Jaworski, *The RESPA Soap Opera Continues for Another Year*, 53 BUS. LAW. 995, 997 (1998).

With respect to nonresidential promissory notes that are negotiable in form, no notice is literally required even when an actual transfer of the note to a new holder occurs. *See* Dale A. Whitman, *Reforming the Law: The Payment Rule as a Paradigm*, 1998 BYU L. REV. 1169 (1998). However, it would be extremely foolish for a lender to transfer the note and fail to notify the borrower, unless the original lender retained the authority to service the loan. The potential for missed payments and much confusion and unhappiness is apparent. Thus, paragraph 32 states what common sense would dictate—that the borrower will be notified of any transfer of servicing.

Single Asset Borrower

Until the Indebtedness is paid in full, Borrower (a) shall not acquire any real or personal property other than the Mortgaged Property and personal property related to the operation and maintenance of the Mortgaged Property; (b) shall not operate any business other than the management and operation of the Mortgaged Property; and (c) shall not maintain its assets in a way difficult to segregate and identify.

Explanation

A major goal of modern lenders on income-producing properties is to make their loans "bankruptcy remote." This is desirable from the lender's viewpoint because the lender does not wish to see the real estate become part of a bankruptcy estate (with its concomitant delays, legal expenses, and potential limitations on foreclosure of the mortgage) because some *other* projects or business activities of the borrower have failed or become insolvent. To accomplish this, most income-producing projects are owned and operated by a special-purpose vehicle (SPV)—an entity that owns just one project. Paragraph 33 of the Deed of Trust seeks to require that the relationship between the SPV and this project be kept pure from entanglement with other projects that the lender has not underwritten, but that might drag this project into bankruptcy.

Even if bankruptcy is filed, the lender who has a single-asset borrower may have an advantage. Under the Bankruptcy Code, a single-asset real estate borrower receives accelerated bankruptcy proceedings if the borrower has no more than $4 million in real property secured debt. See John C. Murray, *The Lender's Guide to Single Asset Real Estate Bankruptcies*, 31 REAL PROP. PROB. & TR. J. 393 (1996). See also supra Section 22, paragraph 22(c).

The issuers of mortgage-backed securities and the rating agencies that evaluate such securitizations particularly insist upon bankruptcy remoteness. A simple "single-asset borrower" clause like the one above is not considered a sufficient assurance of bankruptcy remoteness by these entities. They commonly take other steps as well, including the following: covenants against mergers and consolidations of the borrower entity; "entity controls" such as lender-designated board members and voting trusts designed to prevent the management of the borrower entity from filing a voluntary petition in bankruptcy; "springing" guaranties by the borrower's principals that take effect only in the event of a bankruptcy filing; and the use of a "hard lockbox" system for loan payments, with tenants depositing rents directly into an account controlled by the lender. See Frederick Z. Lodge et al., "Bankruptcy Remote Structures in Mortgage Loans," PROB. & PROP., May/June 1996, at 49. However, paragraph 33 of the Deed of Trust does not provide for use of any of these devices. The effectiveness of these techniques is still largely untested in the courts, and at this point it is clear that "bankruptcy remote" does not necessarily mean "bankruptcy proof." See Michael J. Cohn, *Asset Securitization: How Remote Is Bankruptcy Remote?*, 26 HOFSTRA L. REV. 929 (1998).

Successors and Assigns Bound

This Instrument shall bind, and the rights granted by this Instrument shall inure to, the respective successors and assigns of Lender and Borrower. However, a Transfer not permitted by Section 21 shall be an Event of Default.

Explanation

Transfer by the lender. When the mortgage lender assigns a mortgage and note, the assignee becomes entitled to enforce the borrower's obligations. That is the essential purpose of the assignment of the loan. Whether the lender's *duties* also become binding on the assignee is largely an untested question. The reason is that, unless the loan calls for future advances, the lender typically has no further duties once it has disbursed the loan proceeds.

Transfer by the borrower. On the borrower's side, however, an assignment (i.e., a transfer of the real estate) raises a fascinating (and again, largely untested) question. Clearly, if the transferee of the real estate enters into an assumption agreement, the lender can enforce that agreement as a third-party beneficiary. *See* RESTATEMENT (THIRD) OF PROPERTY: MORTGAGES § 5.1(b)(3) and cmt. d (1997). However, suppose there is no assumption agreement. Is it possible for the lender to argue that the purchaser of the real estate nonetheless becomes automatically and personally liable on the covenants in the note and mortgage, on the ground that the covenants "run with the land"? The answer with respect to the covenant to pay the debt itself is clearly negative; it is well established that a nonassuming purchaser of the mortgaged property has no personal liability on the debt. *See* Schram v. Coyne, 127 F.2d 205 (6th Cir. 1942); RESTATEMENT (THIRD) OF PROPERTY: MORTGAGES § 5.2(d) and cmt. b (1997).

However, what of other covenants found in the mortgage itself? Might they "run with the land" and become the personal liability of the new owner of the land? It seems quite arguable that they could do so, particularly if they were sufficiently related to the real estate that they could be viewed as "touching and concerning" the land. The Reporters' Note to Restatement (Third) of Property: Mortgages § 5.2 comments as follows:

> [C]ase authority on the point is extremely meager, and all of the reported cases deal with covenants to pay ground rent or taxes, breaches of which might well be considered waste even if the covenant's burden did not run with the real estate. *See* Union Trust Co. v. Rosenburg, 189 A.421 (Md. Ct. App. 1937) (covenant to pay taxes); Jones v. Burgess, 4 A.2d 473 (Md. Ct. App. 1939) (covenants to pay ground rent and taxes); McKinnon v. Bradley, 165 P.2d 286 (Or. 1946) (covenant to pay taxes). By analogy, see Esplendido Apartments v. Metropolitan Condominium Ass'n, 778 P.2d 1221 (Ariz. 1989), holding that a due-on-sale clause "ran with the land" and bound a non-assuming grantee; but the mortgagee's remedy in that situation was acceleration and foreclosure, not damages against the grantee. *See generally* Leipziger, The Mortgagee's Remedies for Waste, 64 Cal. L. Rev. 1087, 1133–35 (1976), suggesting that the absence of horizontal privity of estate between mortgagee and original mortgagor might be a barrier to the running of such covenants. . . . Moreover, privity is not required when the plaintiff seeks an equitable remedy for breach of a covenant.

In light of the uncertainty of this issue, what is the relevance of paragraph 34 of the Deed of Trust? Plainly, the parties cannot make mortgage covenants "run with the land" merely by saying so. Nevertheless, the quoted clause should at least be enough to convince a court that the parties *intended* for the covenants to run, thus satisfying one of the traditional elements of running covenants. Whether the other traditional elements— such as horizontal privity of estate (required in order to make the burden run in an action for damages) and the requirement that the covenant "touch and concern" the land—would be found, or whether modern courts would hold that a covenant runs without regard to these elements, remains unclear. The Restatement (Third) of Property: Servitudes purports to abolish the privity and "touch and concern" requirements. RESTATEMENT (THIRD) OF PROPERTY: SERVITUDES § 2.4 (privity requirement abolished), § 3.2 (touch and concern requirement abolished).

Joint and Several Liability

If more than one person or entity signs this Instrument as Borrower, the obligations of such persons and entities shall be joint and several.

Explanation

Liabilities of co-borrowers. Paragraph 35 of the Deed of Trust provides that the liability of the borrower is both joint and several when the borrower is more than one person or entity. There are consequences to this designation. From the lender's perspective, it can sue one and/or the other co-borrower for the full loan balance because each co-borrower agreed to be "severally" liable. Hence, one co-borrower cannot prevent a suit for the full loan balance on the basis that the lender must at the same time sue and attempt to recover from the other co-borrower. *See, e.g.*, Estate of Isaacson v. Hertz, 225 N.E.2d 106 (Ill. App. 1967). However, because liability is also "joint," if the lender has in fact recovered more than one-half of the total debt from one of the co-borrowers, that co-borrower can sue the other co-borrower for contribution of any amounts paid in excess of its share. *See, e.g.*, Shuttleworth v. Abramo, 1993 WL 104552 (Del. Ch. 1993); Estate of Leinbach v. Leinbach, 486 N.E.2d 2 (Ind. App. 1985).

The joint and several nature of the loan furthers the lender's goal to recover its entire investment after the borrower's default as quickly and cheaply as possible. The provision also generally conforms to the co-borrowers' expectation that ultimately they will be responsible only for their share of the liability for the loan. However, to the extent that the mortgaged property is inadequate to pay the debt and one of the co-borrowers has inadequate assets to pay its share of the debt, then it is the co-borrower who will absorb this loss (and the cost of suing other co-borrowers) rather than the lender.

Relationship of Parties; No Third Party Beneficiary

The relationship between Lender and Borrower shall be solely that of creditor and debtor, respectively, and nothing contained in this Instrument shall create any other relationship between Lender and Borrower.

No creditor of any party to this Instrument and no other person shall be a third party beneficiary of this Instrument or any other Loan Document. Without limiting the generality of the preceding sentence, (1) any arrangement (a *"Servicing Arrangement"*) between the Lender and any Loan Servicer for loss sharing or interim advancement of funds shall constitute a contractual obligation of such Loan Servicer that is independent of the obligation of Borrower for the payment of the Indebtedness, (2) Borrower shall not be a third party beneficiary of any Servicing Arrangement, and (3) no payment by the Loan Servicer under any Servicing Arrangement will reduce the amount of the Indebtedness.

Explanation

Debtor/creditor or fiduciary? The first sentence of paragraph 36 of the Deed of Trust should help a lender avoid the charge that it had a fiduciary or other relationship of trust with the borrower. In a number of "lender liability" cases, borrowers have argued that such a relationship existed and that (as a result) the lender had a duty to restructure the loan payments or to delay foreclosure. Courts have nearly always rejected

175

these arguments in cases involving commercial borrowers. *See, e.g.,* Teachers Ins. & Annuity Ass'n v. La Salle Nat'l Bank, 691 N.E.2d 881 (Ill. App. 1998). Nonetheless, the express contractual stipulation in paragraph 36 may help the lender overcome any argument that it had a fiduciary relationship with the borrower.

Underwriting and servicing arrangements. Fannie Mae operates a Delegated Underwriting and Servicing (DUS) program under which some lenders have authority to underwrite and fund mortgage loans meeting certain guidelines, with the assurance that Fannie Mae will purchase the loans on the secondary market. Lenders who use this program can provide faster loan processing and avoid detailed scrutiny by Fannie Mae during the loan origination process. In return, however, these lenders must enter into a "loss sharing" agreement with Fannie Mae, under which the lenders will pay to Fannie Mae a portion of any shortfall in debt service payments made by their borrowers. The lender also services the loans under this arrangement.

In *Dacon Bolingbrook Assocs. Ltd. Partnership. v. Federal Nat'l Mortgage Ass'n,* 155 B.R. 467 (N.D. Ill. 1993), the lender entered into a DUS agreement with Fannie Mae. When the borrower defaulted in payments, the lender made up the deficiency as required by the agreement. Subsequently, when it became apparent that the borrower would not cure the default, Fannie Mae and the lender entered into a settlement agreement that refunded part of the payments the lender had made under the DUS agreement and terminated any further liability of the lender.

The borrower filed bankruptcy, and Fannie Mae was its only secured creditor. In addition to the unpaid principal, Fannie Mae asserted that it had a secured claim for accrued interest at a "default" rate, and that it was entitled to late fees. The borrower argued, by way of defense, that there had been no default because Fannie Mae had actually received all of the payments owed to it, even though it admitted that the lender had made the payments for a lengthy time period.

The court rejected the borrower's position. It pointed out that there was no agreement between the borrower and the lender—and no duty owed by the lender to the borrower—that compelled the lender to make the payments to Fannie Mae. The lender's payments, it held, "in no way constituted payment on behalf of the debtor so as to cure any default." Paragraph 36 of the Deed of Trust is designed to confirm and strengthen the court's holding in the *Dacon Bolingbrook* case, by emphasizing that the lender's duty under such a DUS agreement does not benefit the borrower.

Construction lending. There are other situations in which mortgage agreements may provide expressly that there shall be no third-party beneficiaries. For example, construction lenders sometimes disburse funds in a careless manner, without verifying that the labor and materials associated with a particular disbursement have actually been expended on the job site. When such a negligent disbursement occurs, junior lien holders (e.g., mechanics' lienors, second mortgagees, etc.) who are harmed by the subsequent foreclosure of the construction loan may sue the construction lender. To assert that the lender had a duty of careful disbursement to them, they may claim that they are third-party beneficiaries of the construction loan agreement. Nearly all of the cases considering this claim have rejected it, usually on the ground that the parties to the construction loan agreement did not intend to benefit junior lien holders. *See, e.g.,* Home Sav. Ass'n v. State Bank, 763 F. Supp. 292 (N.D. Ill. 1991); Rockhill v. United States, 418 A.2d 197 (Md. 1980). To strengthen their position, construction lenders usually incorporate language in their construction loan agreements expressly providing that there are no third-party beneficiaries. *See, e.g.,* Inversiones Immobiliarias Internacionales de Orlando Sociedad Anomia v. Barnett Bank, 584 So. 2d 110 (Fla. App. 1991) (upholding such a disclaimer of third-party beneficiaries).

Severability; Amendments

The invalidity or unenforceability of any provision of this Instrument shall not affect the validity or enforceability of any other provision, and all other provisions shall remain in full force and effect. This Instrument contains the entire agreement among the parties as to the rights granted and the obligations assumed in this Instrument. This Instrument may not be amended or modified except by a writing signed by the party against whom enforcement is sought.

Explanation

Severability. The first sentence of paragraph 37 of the Deed of Trust provides that in the event a portion of the loan documents is found to be invalid, the remainder of the loan documents will be enforced. This sentence, sometimes referred to as a "partial invalidity" clause, is important because it is possible that there are some unenforceable provisions among the hundreds of terms embodied in the numerous loan documents typically used to evidence and secure a mortgage loan. One obvious example is the level of interest charged (including late charges and default interest) and the possibility that this might violate usury laws or constitute an unenforceable penalty. *See supra* Section 25.

There is authority to enforce a partial invalidity clause. *See, e.g.,* United Nat'l Bank of Miami v. Airport Plaza Ltd. Partnership, 537 So. 2d 608 (Fla. App. 1988). If the invalid portion of the agreement does

179

not pertain to the essence of the agreement and can be severed as distinct and separate from the rest of the agreement, then the rest of the agreement can be enforced. *Id.* at 611.

Integration.   The second sentence of paragraph 37 provides that the Deed of Trust reflects the complete agreement of the parties, and the third sentence states that no amendments to the loan documents will be effective unless they are in writing. The second sentence, to the extent relating to oral agreements made at or prior to the signing of the loan documents, is referred to as an "integration" clause. It is very helpful to clarify that the words contained in the loan documents constitute the entire agreement of the parties; doing so reduces the likelihood of fraud or misunderstanding as to the parameters of "the deal." Requiring that future modifications to the loan be in writing serves the same function.

There is significant authority to enforce an integration clause. *See, e.g.,* Boulevard Bank Nat'l Ass'n v. Adams Newspapers, Inc., 787 F. Supp. 122, 124 (E.D. Mich. 1992); Wilson v. Landstrom, 315 S.E.2d 130 (S.C. App. 1984).

Post-agreement modification.   While there is ample authority for the enforcement of partial invalidity clauses and integration clauses as found in paragraph 37, any alleged oral modification of the agreement made after the agreement is entered into is not covered by an integration clause. *Wilson,* 315 S.E.2d at 134. Nevertheless, paragraph 37 can be interpreted to express the intent that alleged oral modifications made after the agreement is entered into should not be enforceable. In the absence of a claim of fraud or similar equitable arguments such as estoppel, one could predict that a court would enforce such an agreement, though research indicates no cases on the point. Indeed, any oral agreements relating to interests in real estate may be unenforceable under the statute of frauds as well, unless falling within an exception to the statute.

Construction

*The captions and headings of the sections of this Instrument are for conven-
ience only and shall be disregarded in construing this Instrument. Any reference in this Instrument to an "Exhibit" or a "Section" shall, unless otherwise
explicitly provided, be construed as referring, respectively, to an Exhibit attached to this Instrument or to a Section of this Instrument. All Exhibits attached to or referred to in this Instrument are incorporated by reference into
this Instrument. Any reference in this Instrument to a statute or regulation
shall be construed as referring to that statute or regulation as amended from
time to time. Use of the singular in this Agreement includes the plural and use
of the plural includes the singular. As used in this Instrument, the term "including" means "including, but not limited to."*

Explanation

Captions.   Paragraph 38 of the Deed of Trust clarifies the parties' intent
for the words of the provisions of the Deed of Trust, rather than the captions or heading labels, to control the document's meaning. This can be
helpful, because it is possible for a caption or heading to be deemed inconsistent with the words of the provisions of the loan documents. In
one case, the words in a listing agreement reflected an intent for an
"open listing" (the broker earns her commission if she is the procuring
cause of the sale), but the caption to the agreement stated "exclusive

listing." The court indicated that this created an ambiguity requiring an investigation of parol evidence to ascertain the true meaning of the contract. Neece v. A.A.A. Realty Co., 322 S.W.2d 597, 601-602 (Tex. 1959). *Neece* involved an apparent mistake and a question as to whether the parties intended the type of listing described in the caption or as expressed in the words that followed the caption. Paragraph 38 presumes that if any "mistakes" are made they will be in the caption rather than in the words following the caption.

In *Neece*, the court stated that a court must give greater weight to the operative contractual clauses of the contract than to the label used in the contract. Thus, language such as that in paragraph 38 should help direct a court to focus on the operative contractual provisions rather than the captions and headings themselves in the event of any inconsistency. Nevertheless, a court might still decide to look at parol evidence to prevent fraud and in such case, depending upon the parol evidence, may interpret the ambiguity in a fashion consistent with the caption or heading.

Other interpretive issues.   Paragraph 38 clarifies three other points that are not controversial at the onset of the loan but that, if not clarified, could arise as a source of dispute after the loan is made: (i) that the exhibits attached to the agreement are incorporated by reference into the agreement (indeed, the signature page of the Deed of Trust even lists the attached exhibits), (ii) that all references to statutes and regulations imply the statutes and regulations as amended from time to time, and (iii) that the term "including" means "including, but not limited to" (to avoid the claim that what has been enumerated is exhaustive).

Loan Servicing

All actions regarding the servicing of the loan evidenced by the Note, including the collection of payments, the giving and receipt of notice, inspections of the Property, inspections of books and records, and the granting of consents and approvals, may be taken by the Loan Servicer unless Borrower receives notice to the contrary. If Borrower receives conflicting notices regarding the identity of the Loan Servicer or any other subject, any such notice from Lender shall govern.

Explanation

For a discussion of the functions of servicers, *see supra* Section 32. Paragraph 39 of the Deed of Trust confirms to the borrower that the lender's designated servicer has authority to perform all of the acts mentioned. It also clarifies the lender's authority to resolve any possible dispute as to what entity is the designated servicer.

Disclosure of
Information

Lender may furnish information regarding Borrower or the Mortgaged Property to third parties with an existing or prospective interest in the servicing, enforcement, evaluation, performance, purchase or securitization of the Indebtedness, including trustees, master servicers, special servicers, rating agencies, and organizations maintaining databases on the underwriting and performance of multifamily mortgage loans. Borrower irrevocably waives any and all rights it may have under applicable law to prohibit such disclosure, including any right of privacy.

Explanation

Confidentiality of information regarding the borrower and mortgaged property. The advent of widespread securitization of commercial mortgage loans has produced vast changes in borrowers' expectations of privacy and confidentiality. No longer can a borrower reasonably anticipate that the lender will keep secret the details of a loan transaction. The disclosure requirements of the securities laws dictate that, when a loan is placed in a securitized pool, prospective investors and those who represent them (REMIC trustees, servicers, and rating agencies) must receive complete access to all details of the transaction. Further, the borrower's performance under the loan (including delinquencies and any breaches of mortgage covenants) also becomes an open book.

185

Fannie Mae includes paragraph 40 in the Deed of Trust in order to warn the borrower of the required disclosure practices and to ward off any claim that such disclosures are violations of the borrower's privacy or confidentiality rights.

No Change in Facts or Circumstances

*All information in the application for the loan submitted to Lender (the **"Loan Application"**) and in all financial statements, rent rolls, reports, certificates and other documents submitted in connection with the Loan Application are complete and accurate in all material respects. There has been no material adverse change in any fact or circumstance that would make any such information incomplete or inaccurate.*

Explanation

The lender's "due diligence" investigation. Lenders generally decide to fund a mortgage loan based on the accuracy of certain financial and legal information about the borrower and the mortgaged property. This information may include, among other things, the borrower's most recent certified or uncertified financial statements, the most current rent roll for the premises, existing leases, expense reports, and/or certificates of occupancy. If this information overstates the borrower's financial strength or the profitability of the operations of the property, the lender may overvalue the property and make an imprudent loan.

Traditionally, a prudent lender will not rely entirely upon the accuracy of the information in the borrower's loan application and accompanying documents, but will undertake its own "due diligence" investigation to confirm the accuracy of that information. If a due diligence investigation reveals that the borrower's information is inaccurate, the lender can refuse to advance the loan or do so on different terms that take into account the correct information and the appropriate risk characteristics of the loan. Unfortunately, even a prudent due diligence investigation will not always reveal material inaccuracies or changed circumstances. For example, the borrower may have systematically understated its recorded maintenance expenses in order to overstate the profitability of the premises and justify a higher loan amount. If the lender does not discover the understatement, the lender may underwrite the loan at an unjustified loan amount.

Reasons for a "no material adverse changes" statement. For the above reasons, a prudent lender will want the borrower to state without equivocation that all information submitted for the lender's consideration is accurate and complete in all material respects. Paragraph 41 of the Deed of Trust contains a representation suitable for this purpose. How does paragraph 41 improve the lender's position?

- First, a material misrepresentation or omission in the application materials constitutes not only a breach of the representation in paragraph 41 but also an event of default under paragraph 22(d), thereby authorizing the lender to take immediate action, without further demand, to accelerate the maturity of the debt under paragraph 43. *The misrepresentation need not be fraudulent;* a negligent misrepresentation or omission would constitute an event of default if it was material.

- Second, if the loan is a nonrecourse loan, a material misrepresentation or omission (whether fraudulent or negligent) in the application materials will deprive the borrower—at least in part—of the benefit of the nonrecourse provisions of the Form Note. If the lender was damaged by a material misrepresentation or omission in the application materials, paragraph 9(b) of the Note would permit the lender to recover personally against the borrower to the extent of the loss suffered by the lender. For example, suppose the borrower understated its operating expenses, thereby inflating the valuation of the mortgaged premises by $500,000. As a result, the lender loans $375,000 (at a 75 percent loan-to-value ratio) more than it would have loaned against the mortgaged premises if the lender had known of the correct information. Even if the loan was otherwise nonrecourse, the lender could obtain a judgment against the borrower in the amount of $375,000 under paragraph 9(b) of the note. *See supra* Section 6.

- Third, to the extent that the loan is a nonrecourse loan, a material misrepresentation or omission in the loan application gives the lender a legal basis to challenge the borrower's ability to discharge its personal liability on the debt in a bankruptcy proceeding. Under Bankruptcy Code § 523(a)(2), bankruptcy would not discharge a debt where the borrower obtained credit by means of a *written* statement that was (1) materially false, (2) in regard to the borrower's financial condition, (3) reasonably relied upon by the lender in extending credit, and (4) made with the intent to deceive.

Bankruptcy courts typically have concluded that the omission, concealment, or understatement of significant liabilities (actual or contingent) constitutes a materially false statement. *See e.g., In re* Poskanzer, 143 B.R. 991 (Bankr. D.N.J. 1992); *In re* Woolum, 979 F.2d 71, 76 (6th Cir. 1992). Statements concerning the ownership of assets clearly qualify as statements regarding a debtor's financial condition. *In re* Boice, 149 B.R. 40 (Bankr. S.D.N.Y. 1992).

Whether the lender's reliance on a borrower's false statement or omission is reasonable is a function of all of the relevant facts and circumstances, including (a) any previous dealings between the lender and the borrower, (b) any warnings that may have alerted a prudent person to the borrower's misstatements, (c) evidence that minimal investigation would have revealed the misstatements, and (d) the lender's standard practices in evaluating the creditworthiness of its borrowers and the customs and practices of the lending industry. 4 COLLIER ON BANKRUPTCY ¶ 523.08[2][d] at 523–49 (15th ed.). Evidence tending to prove that the lender would not have made the loan had it received accurate information is sufficient to demonstrate reliance. *In re* Coughlin, 27 B.R. 632 (B.A.P. 1st Cir. 1983). The lender's claims to reliance cannot be so unreasonable as to defeat a finding of reliance in fact. *In re* Woolum, 979 F.2d 71, 76 (6th Cir. 1992); *In re* Garman, 643 F.2d 1252, 1258 (7th Cir. 1980).

To deprive the borrower of the ability to discharge its personal liability on the debt, the misstatement or omission must have been made with the intent to deceive; mere negligence is not sufficient. The lender must show that the statement was either knowingly false or made so recklessly as to justify a finding that the borrower acted fraudulently. *In re* Batie, 995 F.2d 85 (6th Cir. 1993); *In re* Black, 787 F.2d 503 (10th Cir. 1986).

Subrogation

*If, and to the extent that, the proceeds of the loan evidenced by the Note are used to pay, satisfy or discharge any obligation of Borrower for the payment of money that is secured by a pre-existing mortgage, deed of trust or other lien encumbering the Mortgaged Property (a **"Prior Lien"**), such loan proceeds shall be deemed to have been advanced by Lender at Borrower's request, and Lender shall automatically, and without further action on its part, be subrogated to the rights, including lien priority, of the owner or holder of the obligation secured by the Prior Lien, whether or not the Prior Lien is released.*

Explanation

Equitable subrogation. The principle of equitable subrogation dictates that, when a lender makes a loan whose proceeds are used to pay an existing mortgage debt of the borrower, the lender is entitled to step into the shoes of the creditor who was paid and to become the holder of the mortgage that was paid. *See* RESTATEMENT (THIRD) OF PROPERTY: MORTGAGES § 7.6(b)(4) (1997). In effect, the mortgage is assigned to the paying lender by operation of law. This principle is particularly useful to the paying lender when it later develops that there was, unknown to the paying lender, an intervening lien.

To illustrate, assume that a piece of land is subject to two mortgages, held by ME1 and ME2, with ME1 having priority. The borrower

191

approaches a new lender, ME3, and arranges a loan to "refinance" the ME1 debt. ME3 makes that loan, and its entire proceeds are disbursed to pay ME1's debt in full. ME3 has no actual knowledge of the fact that the ME2 mortgage encumbers the land; instead, ME3 assumes that, when ME1's mortgage is discharged, ME3 will have the only mortgage on the land. However, after the payoff of ME1 is completed, ME2 asserts that its mortgage has now been promoted to first priority above ME3's.

If the principle of equitable subrogation is applied, ME3 will be permitted to step into ME1's shoes. Thus, ME3 will be regarded as holding the ME1 mortgage and hence will have priority over ME2 to the extent that the funds advanced by ME3 were applied to pay off ME1. This result is beneficial to ME3, giving it the priority it expected to have. At the same time, the result is not unfairly detrimental to ME2, because it simply leaves ME2's priority unchanged. Indeed, in the absence of subrogation, ME2 would receive an undeserved and unexpected promotion to first priority.

Paragraph 42 of the Deed of Trust is designed to encourage courts to use the subrogation doctrine if the proceeds of the mortgage loan are used to pay off a preexisting mortgage debt. The use of loan proceeds for this purpose is very common; perhaps the most obvious illustration is the retirement of a construction loan mortgage with the proceeds of a long-term or "permanent" loan. In this setting, subrogation may be extremely useful to the long-term lender in gaining priority over intervening mechanics' liens, for example.

Unfortunately, the courts are divided as to the extent to which the paying lender must lack notice in order to have the benefits of subrogation. The view of the Restatement, supported by a few courts, is that subrogation should be recognized even if the paying lender had actual knowledge of the intervening lien, provided that the paying lender "reasonably expected to receive a security interest in the real estate with the priority of the mortgage being discharged." RESTATEMENT (THIRD) OF PROPERTY: MORTGAGES § 7.6(b)(4); Klotz v. Klotz, 440 N.W.2d 406 (Iowa App. 1989); East Boston Savings Bank v. Ogan, 701 N.E.2d 331 (Mass. 1998); Farm Credit Bank v. Ogden, 886 S.W.2d 305 (Tex. App. 1994). A second view, taken in the majority of decisions, is that the paying lender will qualify for subrogation if it has no actual notice of the intervening lien, even though that lien may have been recorded and hence imparted constructive notice. See United States v. Baran, 996 F.2d 25 (2d Cir. 1993) (N.Y. law); First Fidelity Bank v. Travelers Mortgage Services, Inc., 693 A.2d 525 (N.J. Super. 1997); R.C.P.S.

Associates v. Karam Developers, 656 N.Y.S.2d 666 (App. Div. 1997); Han v. United States, 944 F.2d 526 (9th Cir. 1991) (California law). Finally, a small group of states disqualify the paying lender for subrogation even if it had only constructive notice from the recordation of the intervening lien. *See In re* Gordon, 164 B.R. 706 (Bankr. S.D. Fla. 1994) (Florida law); Independence One Mortgage Corp. v. Katsaros, 681 A.2d 1005 (Conn. App. 1996).

Paragraph 42 of the Deed of Trust makes no specific reference to the lender's knowledge or notice of any intervening lien. Hence, if the clause is taken literally, even if the lender has actual knowledge of an intervening lien, the lender will gain priority over that lien when it pays off a superior mortgage. However, whether the courts will take the clause literally and disregard the lender's actual notice of the intervening lien is uncertain. There is considerable authority that subrogation will be granted, even if the paying lender has actual knowledge of the intervening lien, if the paying lender has entered into an agreement with either the borrower or the party whose lien is being paid, granting it subrogation to the paid lien. This notion, based on express agreement, is termed "conventional subrogation." *See* G. NELSON & D. WHITMAN, REAL ESTATE FINANCE LAW § 10.1 (3d ed. 1994). For example, in *First Fidelity Bank v. Travelers Mortgage Services, Inc.*, 693 A.2d 525 (N.J. Super. 1997), the court observed:

> Where a third party loans or advances money to pay off a mortgage pursuant to an agreement with the owner of the redemption interest that the third party lender shall have the benefit of the mortgage as security for his loan, he is clearly entitled to keep the mortgage alive and to enforce it against junior encumbrances even if he does not obtain an assignment of the mortgage.

It is thus entirely possible that a court would accept the mortgage clause above as a sufficient agreement to actuate the doctrine of conventional subrogation and hence would grant subrogation irrespective of the paying lender's knowledge. However, the prudent course for the lender is to obtain a title insurance policy that insures the priority of the mortgage. If that is done, it will be the title insurance company—not the lender—that will make the argument for subrogation.

Acceleration; Remedies

At any time during the existence of an Event of Default, Lender, at Lender's option, may declare the Indebtedness to be immediately due and payable without further demand, and may invoke the power of sale and any other remedies permitted by Virginia law or provided in this Instrument or in any other Loan Document. Borrower acknowledges that the power of sale granted by this Instrument may be exercised by Lender without prior judicial hearing. Borrower has the right to bring an action to assert that an Event of Default does not exist or to raise any other defense Borrower may have to acceleration and sale. Lender shall be entitled to collect all costs and expenses incurred in pursuing such remedies, including attorneys' fees and costs of documentary evidence, abstracts and title reports.

If Lender invokes the power of sale, Lender or Trustee shall deliver a copy of a notice of sale to Borrower in the manner prescribed by Virginia law. Trustee shall give public notice of the sale in the manner prescribed by Virginia law and shall sell the Mortgaged Property in accordance with Virginia law. Trustee, without demand on Borrower, shall sell the Mortgaged Property at public auction to the highest bidder at the time and place and under the terms designated in the notice of sale in one or more parcels and in such order as Trustee may determine. Trustee may postpone the sale of all or any part of the Mortgaged Property by public announcement at the time and place of any previously scheduled sale or by advertising in accordance with

Virginia law. Lender or Lender's designee may purchase the Mortgaged Property at any sale.

Trustee shall deliver to the purchaser at the sale, within a reasonable time after the sale, a deed conveying the Mortgaged Property so sold with special warranty of title. The recitals in the Trustee's deed shall be prima facie evidence of the truth of the statements made in the recitals. Trustee shall apply the proceeds of the sale in the following order: (a) to all costs and expenses of the sale, including Trustee's fees of ____% of the gross sale price, attorneys' fees and costs of title evidence; (b) to the discharge of all Taxes, if any, as provided by Virginia law; (c) to the Indebtedness in such order as Lender, in Lender's discretion, directs; and (d) the excess, if any, to the person or persons legally entitled to the excess, including, if any, the holders of liens inferior to this Instrument in the order of their priority, provided that Trustee has actual notice of such liens. Trustee shall not be required to take possession of the Mortgaged Property before the sale or to deliver possession of the Mortgaged Property to the purchaser at the sale.

Explanation

Paragraph 43 of the Deed of Trust addresses a variety of issues associated with the lender's decision to accelerate the maturity of the mortgage debt following default by the borrower. Each of the different issues raised by paragraph 43 is addressed below.

When does the lender's acceleration take effect? Can the lender accelerate the maturity of the mortgage debt without notice to or demand of the borrower?   Courts have used a variety of rules to determine when acceleration of a mortgage debt becomes effective pursuant to an acceleration clause in the mortgage. Most courts have held that the mortgagee must perform some overt affirmative act demonstrating an intention to accelerate the mortgage debt, but that this act need not involve notice to the mortgagor prior to acceleration. *See, e.g.,* Butter v. Melrose Savings Bank, 435 N.E.2d 1057 (Mass. App. 1982) (requirement satisfied by a letter to mortgagor stating that acceleration had already occurred); United States Savings Bank of Newark v. Continental Arms, Inc., 338 A.2d 579 (Del. Super. 1975) (institution of judicial foreclosure proceeding constituted sufficient evidence of an election to accelerate mortgage debt). In contrast, courts in Texas have required the mortgagee to give the mortgagor *both* notice of intent to accelerate prior to acceleration *and* a separate notice of the acceleration itself. *See, e.g.,* Ogden v. Gibraltar Savings Ass'n, 640 S.W.2d 232 (Tex. 1982);

McLemore v. Pacific Southwest Bank, FSB, 872 S.W.2d 286 (Tex. App. 1994). In the view of these courts, a separate, pre-acceleration notice of the intent to accelerate is "necessary in order to provide the debtor an opportunity to cure his default prior to the harsh consequences of acceleration and foreclosure." *Ogden*, 640 S.W.2d at 234. Furthermore, the Texas courts have held that provisions in the loan documents allowing the mortgagee to accelerate "without prior notice or demand" are not effective to waive the mortgagor's right to notice of intention to accelerate prior to acceleration. *See, e.g.*, Shumway v. Horizon Credit Corp., 801 S.W.2d 890 (Tex. 1991).

The new Restatement (Third) of Property: Mortgages has attempted to provide some clarity by providing that "[a]n acceleration becomes effective on the date specified in a written notice by the mortgagee to the mortgagor delivered after default." RESTATEMENT (THIRD) OF PROPERTY: MORTGAGES § 8.1(a). Under this approach, the mortgagee must provide one (but not more than one) written notice after the mortgagor's default; the notice can specify that the acceleration is effective either upon delivery of the notice or at a later date specified in the notice. Further, the Restatement takes the position that the mortgage loan documents may not waive this written notice requirement. *Id.* § 8.1, comment b.

One might argue that, on its face, paragraph 43 of the Deed of Trust would permit the lender to accelerate the maturity of the mortgage debt without notice to or demand of the borrower. (Of course, a subsequent judicial foreclosure would require notice to the borrower in order to obtain personal jurisdiction over the borrower, and a subsequent power-of-sale foreclosure would require notice of the sale to the borrower in order to satisfy the statute authorizing power-of-sale foreclosure.) Under this view, paragraph 43 would be sufficient to allow the lender to accelerate the maturity of the mortgage debt without a separate pre-acceleration notice to the borrower, as long as the lender performs some additional act (such as instituting a foreclosure process) that evidences the lender's decision to accelerate the debt. One might also argue, however, that paragraph 43's use of the language "Lender . . . may *declare* the Indebtedness to be immediately due and payable" suggests that the lender must make a declaration to the borrower in the form of a written notice such as that contemplated by Restatement § 8.1. In a jurisdiction that adopts the Restatement view, the lender would thus be obligated to provide the borrower with written notice that it had accelerated the debt. In a jurisdiction such as Texas, it is doubtful that paragraph 43 would be sufficient to waive the borrower's right to notice prior to acceleration.

In any event, regardless of whether the mortgage documents require notice prior to acceleration, the prudent lender generally chooses to provide the borrower with notice and an opportunity to cure prior to acceleration, even if only out of courtesy and/or goodwill rather than any obligation imposed by the loan documents.

Can the borrower reinstate the original maturity of the mortgage debt without paying the full accelerated balance?

Paragraph 43 of the Deed of Trust, tracking the language of the Note, provides no contractual right to reinstate the debt following acceleration. As a result, the borrower could redeem the mortgaged property from the lien created by the Deed of Trust only by paying the full accelerated balance of the mortgage debt, along with any costs, fees, and expenses assessed to the borrower under the terms of the loan documents. This traditional result is reflected in the Restatement (Third) of Property: Mortgages § 8.1(c) ("After an acceleration has taken place . . . a mortgagor may prevent foreclosure only by paying or tendering to the mortgagee the full accelerated mortgage obligation").

A number of states, however, have enacted statutes permitting the mortgagor to reinstate the original maturity of the mortgage debt merely by curing the borrower's arrearages. *See, e.g.,* CAL. CIV. CODE ANN. § 2924c; COLO. REV. STAT. § 38-38-104; MINN. STAT. ANN. § 580.30; UTAH CODE § 57-1-31. In jurisdictions with these "arrearages" statutes, timely cure by the borrower obligates the mortgagee to reinstate the maturity of the debt and cease any further activities in foreclosing the mortgage.

Can the lender/trustee exercise the power of sale without any judicial supervision?

In a number of states, judicial foreclosure is the exclusive method of foreclosing a mortgage lien. 1 G. NELSON & D. WHITMAN, REAL ESTATE FINANCE LAW § 7.11, at 580 (prac. ed. 1993). In such states, foreclosure under the power of sale contained in paragraph 43 is not available.

In those states authorizing power-of-sale foreclosure (approximately 60 percent of the states), the mortgage lender generally may direct the trustee to conduct a sale by complying with the notification requirements contained in the deed of trust and any other notification requirements provided in the statute authorizing power-of-sale foreclosure. In the overwhelming majority of these states, power-of-sale foreclosure occurs without any judicial supervision or proceedings. In these states, paragraph 43 (which authorizes the lender to proceed "without prior judicial hearing") is enforceable according to its terms.

Because most power-of-sale foreclosure statutes do not require a hearing to be conducted prior to sale, some have argued that these power-of-sale foreclosure statutes violate the due process clause of the Fourteenth Amendment. Most courts have rejected this argument, on the ground that the mortgagor has the right to file a lawsuit seeking to enjoin the foreclosure and thus can obtain a hearing prior to sale in that fashion. (As noted above, paragraph 43 recognizes the borrower's right to pursue such an action.) Although commentators have challenged this view, *see* 1 Nelson & Whitman, *supra*, § 7.25, at 650–51, most courts have concluded that the mortgagor's ability to seek judicial relief provides the mortgagor with sufficient opportunity to a hearing prior to sale and thus satisfies the Fourteenth Amendment. *See, e.g.,* Laughlin v. Walters, 718 F.2d 513 (1st Cir. 1983).

In North Carolina, however, the federal district court concluded that North Carolina's power-of-sale foreclosure statute was unconstitutional to the extent that it did not provide for a hearing prior to sale. Turner v. Blackburn, 389 F. Supp. 1250 (W.D.N.C. 1975). In response, the North Carolina legislature amended its power-of-sale foreclosure statute to provide for a pre-sale hearing, conducted before the clerk of the court in the county where the land is located. N.C. Gen. Stat. § 45-21.16. Likewise, in Colorado, judicial process is required prior to sale under power-of-sale foreclosure. Power-of-sale foreclosure in Colorado is conducted by the "public trustee," who must obtain a court order authorizing the sale before the sale may be conducted. Colo. Stat. Ann. § 38-38-105.

Limits on the lender's ability to collect attorneys' fees and expenses of sale. Paragraph 43 of the Deed of Trust authorizes the lender to assess the borrower with the costs of pursuing its post-default remedies. Under the law of most states, such contractual provisions are freely enforceable against the borrower.

A limited number of states have statutory limitations upon the lender's ability to collect attorneys' fees from a defaulting borrower. North Dakota statutes provide that "[a]ny provision contained in any note, bond, mortgage, security agreement, or other evidence of debt for the payment of an attorney's fee in case of default in payment or in proceedings had to collect such note, bond, or evidence of debt, or to foreclose such mortgage or security agreement, is against public policy and void." N.D. Cent. Code § 28-26-04 (1974). Prior to 1994, Kansas law likewise invalidated attorneys' fee provisions in mortgages. Kan. Stat. Ann. § 58-2312. Although a 1994 amendment to § 58-2312 now authorizes the collection of attorneys' fees pursuant to clauses in mortgages, the pre-1994 prohibition still applies to instruments executed before the amendment's effective date. Baxter State

Bank v. Berhnardt, 985 F. Supp. 1259 (D. Kan. 1997). In a few other states, statutes authorize the collection of attorneys' fees only after compliance with procedural "notice and cure period" protections. For example, in North Carolina, a creditor cannot enforce an attorneys' fees clause in a note without first giving the debtor a written "five-day notice" of the creditor's intention to enforce the attorneys' fees clause if the debtor does not repay the debt within that five-day period. If the creditor fails to give this notice, or if the debtor pays within the five-day period, the attorneys' fees provision is unenforceable. N.C. GEN. STAT. § 6-21.2(5). Georgia's notice statute is similar to North Carolina's, except that it expands the notice period to ten days. GA. CODE § 13-1-11(a).

The lender's ability to collect attorneys' fees expended in pursuing its default remedies may also be compromised, despite the express language of paragraph 43, in the event that the borrower files for bankruptcy protection. Under § 506(b) of the Bankruptcy Code, 11 U.S.C. § 506(b), a creditor holding a secured claim against a bankrupt debtor can recover its post-default attorneys' fees only if its claim is oversecured (i.e., only if the value of the collateral exceeds the balance of the creditor's claim). If market fluctuations have caused the mortgaged property to decline in value below the amount of the mortgage debt, the lender would be unable to recover attorneys' fees as a part of its secured claim if the borrower files a bankruptcy petition and its bankruptcy case is not thereafter dismissed.

What notice must the lender provide prior to sale?   Paragraph 43 requires the lender to provide notice of sale to the borrower and also requires the lender to "give public notice of the sale in the manner prescribed by [state] law" and to "sell the Mortgaged Property in accordance with [state] law." Thus, the lender must provide notice of sale to the borrower and to any other person that must receive notice pursuant to the state's power-of-sale foreclosure statute. Power-of-sale foreclosure statutes vary somewhat from state to state regarding the entitlement of parties other than the borrower and the record owner of the land (if different from the borrower) to notice of sale. Some states require that the lender must notify the holders of any junior liens or claims that appear on the public record or are known to the lender. See, e.g., ALASKA STAT. § 34.20.070(c); IDAHO CODE § 45-1506(2)(c). Other states require the lender to notify only those junior claimants who have recorded a request for notice prior to sale. See, e.g., MO. ANN. STAT. § 443.325; N.C. GEN. STAT. § 45-21.17A. Regardless of state law, a power-of-sale foreclosure will not be effective against a subordinate federal tax lien unless the lender gives the United States written notice of sale at least 25 days prior to sale. 26 U.S.C. § 7425(b),(c).

What effect does it have on the sale if the lender fails to provide notice as required?   Some courts have concluded that the failure of the lender/trustee to give notice to the borrower as required by the power-of-sale foreclosure statute renders the sale void. *See, e.g.,* Shearer v. Allied Live Oak Bank, 758 S.W.2d 940 (Tex. App. 1988); Little v. CFS Serv. Corp., 233 Cal. Rptr. 923 (App. 1987). Under this view, the failure to provide notice to the borrower would allow the borrower to set aside the sale even against a bona fide purchaser at the sale. The possibility of collateral attack of foreclosure sales based upon defects in notice, however, has potentially significant consequences for the viability of power-of-sale foreclosure as a remedy. To the extent that foreclosure sale purchasers cannot receive some assurance of finality of title, potential purchasers may be dissuaded from bidding at foreclosure sales, thereby resulting in sales that would systematically produce fewer bidders and lower sale prices.

Legislatures have ameliorated the potential negative effect of notice-of-sale decisions by authorizing the use of trustee's deed recitals as evidence of the trustee's compliance with all statutory requirements. Paragraph 43 of the Deed of Trust provides that "[t]he recitals in the Trustee's deed shall be prima facie evidence of the truth of the statements made in the recitals." If the trustee's deed (as is typical) contains recitals of the trustee's compliance with all statutory requirements governing the foreclosure, the power-of-sale foreclosure statute in most states would make these recitals prima facie evidence of the trustee's compliance. Indeed, in some states these recitals would constitute conclusive evidence of the trustee's compliance in favor of bona fide purchasers or encumbrancers without notice of the defect. *See, e.g.,* UTAH CODE § 57-1-28(1); CAL. CIV. CODE ANN. § 2924; OR. REV. STAT. § 86.780. In other states, these recitals would generally constitute conclusive evidence of the trustee's compliance but would not affect the interest of a person who was entitled to notice but did not receive it. *See, e.g.,* WASH. REV. CODE ANN. § 61.24.070(7).

Sales in bulk versus sales by parcel.   Paragraph 43 of the Deed of Trust provides that the trustee may sell the mortgaged premises "under the terms designated in the notice of sale in one or more parcels and in such order as Trustee may determine." Mortgaged land is often suitable for division into smaller parcels (such as subdivision lots) for purposes of foreclosure as an alternative to sale of the entire tract. If the mortgaged property can be sold either as a whole or in smaller parcels, is the trustee obligated to pursue one method of sale rather than the other?

Some courts have concluded that the party conducting the sale should choose the method of sale most likely to benefit the mortgagor, and that there is thus a presumption in favor of selling in smaller parcels. *See, e.g.,* Garris v. Federal Land Bank of Jackson, 584 So. 2d 791 (Ala. 1991); J.H. Morris v. Indian Hills, Inc., 212 So. 2d 831 (Ala. 1968) (sale in parcels or lots opens the sale to a greater number of bidders and is thus conducive to a better price). In contrast, other courts have concluded that, unless the loan documents provide the trustee with specific direction, the method of sale is within the trustee's discretion, and thus sales in bulk are presumptively valid. *See, e.g.,* Hoer v. Wurdack, 766 S.W.2d 673 (Mo. App. 1989); Classic Enters., Inc. v. Continental Mortgage Investors, 217 S.E.2d 411 (Ga. App. 1975). Furthermore, some courts have held that if the mortgage authorizes sale by either method, this authorization negates the presumption in favor of selling by smaller parcels and validates a bulk sale. *See, e.g.,* McHugh v. Church, 583 P.2d 210 (Alaska 1978); Ames v. Pardue, 389 So. 2d 927 (Ala. 1980).

In a number of states, there is specific statutory regulation of this question. Where the mortgaged premises consist of distinct parcels, some states require that they be sold separately and that all of the parcels cannot be sold if sale of fewer than all the parcels would satisfy the outstanding mortgage balance. *See, e.g.,* MINN. STAT. ANN. § 580.08; N.D. CENT. CODE § 35-22-09. Some states permit the mortgagor to direct sale by smaller parcels where the mortgaged property consists of multiple parcels and such a sale would prove advantageous. *See, e.g.,* UTAH CODE § 57-1-27(1); *see also* ARIZ. REV. STAT. § 33-810 (if mortgagor requests sale by parcels, the trustee shall conditionally sell the property by lots and by whole, and then accept the highest total price).

Absent specific statutory guidance, paragraph 43 should be sufficient to permit the trustee to exercise its discretion to conduct the sale by whichever method it chooses. Where there is any uncertainty as to the proper method of sale, however, it may be prudent for the lender and trustee to advertise and conduct the sale in a conditional fashion, both in bulk and by smaller parcels, with the mortgaged property being finally sold to the highest bidder(s) by the method that produces the highest total sales price. *Cf.* 1 NELSON & WHITMAN, *supra,* § 7.21, at 622.

How extensively must the lender/trustee advertise the sale?   In general, the power-of-sale foreclosure process is somewhat analogous to the secured party's right to repossess and sell personal property under Article 9 of the Uniform Commercial Code. Each regime allows the secured lender to exercise its foreclosure rights in a nonjudicial setting. Nevertheless, Article 9 holds the foreclosing secured party to a higher standard than the one real estate law places upon a mortgagee exercising a power of sale. Under § 9-504(3) of the 1972 text and § 9-610(b) of the 1999 revision, Article 9 requires that the foreclosing secured party conduct a sale that is "commercially reasonable" in every aspect, including "the method, manner, time, place, and other terms." Often, secured parties may publicly advertise foreclosure sales by nothing more than a legal notice in the classified advertisements of a legal or general-circulation newspaper. In some cases involving specialized collateral, however, courts have concluded that foreclosing secured parties must target their advertisements more meaningfully. For example, in *Contrail Leasing Partners, Ltd. v. Consolidated Airways, Inc.*, 742 F.2d 1095 (7th Cir. 1984), the court held that a secured party foreclosing on an airplane breached the "commercially reasonable" standard by running only one inconspicuous advertisement, when a "serious effort to interest potential buyers would have required a more conspicuous ad plus advertising in other trade publications as well." Under this view, the secured party conducting a foreclosure sale should take care to target its advertisement of the sale in a fashion likely to generate meaningful interest in the sale among potential buyers.

In contrast, power-of-sale foreclosure statutes typically do not impose an express duty of "commercial reasonableness" upon the foreclosing mortgagee. Instead, most of the statutes require only that the trustee publish a limited number of notices in newspapers of general circulation in the county where the land is located. *See, e.g.*, MO. STAT. ANN. § 443.320; N.C. GEN. STAT. § 45-21.17. Most courts have concluded that compliance with these minimum statutory requirements is sufficient, even if additional advertisements or advertisements in other forums might have generated wider interest in the sale and thereby might have produced a higher price. For example, Texas courts have held that "a mortgagee is under no duty to take affirmative action, beyond that required by statute or deed of trust, to ensure a 'fair' sale." Pentad Joint Venture v. First Nat'l Bank of La Grange, 797 S.W.2d 72, 76 (Tex. App. 1990). Indeed, the *Pentad* court expressly rejected the view that a foreclosure sale under a deed of trust had to be "commercially reasonable" and held that a failure to conduct a commercially reasonable foreclosure sale of land is not actionable. *See also* Huddleston v. Texas Commerce Bank—Dallas, N.A., 756 S.W.2d 343, 347 (Tex. App. 1988). Under this view, the trustee's compliance with the minimum standards established by the power-of-sale foreclosure statute and the loan documents would insulate the sale from subsequent scrutiny.

Nevertheless, the Mississippi Supreme Court has borrowed the "commercially reasonable" standard from Article 9 and has applied it by analogy to foreclosure by power of sale. In *Wansley v. First Nat'l Bank of Vicksburg*, 566 So. 2d 1218 (Miss. 1990), the court held that every aspect of sale under a power of sale, "including the method, advertising, time, place and terms, must be commercially reasonable." *Wansley*, 566 So. 2d at 1127. Under this view, the requirements established by the statute and the loan documents would establish only a minimum "floor" below which the lender/trustee could not sink; the lender/trustee would also have to take any additional objectively reasonable steps to advertise and conduct the sale in a fashion designed to produce a sale reasonably calculated to produce a fair price for the land. Likewise, in sustaining a judgment for damages against a foreclosing mortgagee who purchased the property at its own sale for a below-market price, the New Hampshire Supreme Court observed that the mortgagee could have "advertised commercially by display advertising in order to assure that bidders other than themselves would be present." Murphy v. Financial Development Corp., 495 A.2d 1245, 1251 (N.H. 1985). The court's suggestion in *Murphy* should give lenders some pause, inasmuch as the mortgagee in that case had complied with all of the statutory requirements for advertising the sale.

Can the lender purchase the mortgaged property at the sale?   Often, foreclosure sales produce little public interest and few (if any) bidders other than the mortgage lender, even in cases where there may exist equity in the land beyond the balance of the mortgage debt. In such a case, a mortgagee might be tempted to credit bid the balance of its debt and (if that remains the high bid) thereby capture any equity in the land for itself. Traditionally, mortgage law—which has been quite protective of the borrower's equitable interest in the mortgaged premises—looked unfavorably upon the potential for abuse inherent in allowing the mortgagee to purchase at its own foreclosure sale. To prevent such abuse, a number of decisions held that, where a mortgage contained a power of sale, the mortgagee exercising that power of sale could not purchase at its own sale. 1 NELSON & WHITMAN, *supra*, § 7.21, at 625.

Such concerns over the potential for mortgagee abuse in the foreclosure process led in part to the development and widespread use of the three-party deed of trust as a substitute for the traditional two-party mortgage. In the three-party deed of trust, the power of sale is vested in an independent third person obligated to conduct the sale in an ostensibly neutral manner—thereby (also ostensibly) addressing or ameliorating concerns about potential mortgagee abuse.

It is hardly clear that the involvement of a trustee necessarily renders the foreclosure process any less susceptible to the potential abuse of mortgagees systematically making low credit bids. Nevertheless, courts and power-of-sale foreclosure statutes have routinely permitted the deed-of-trust beneficiary to purchase mortgaged premises at the sale. *Id.* at 627. Thus, as a general matter, the provisions of paragraph 43 (authorizing the lender to purchase at the sale) should be enforceable.

If the trustee and lender are related, however—as in the case where the trustee is an employee of the lender—the relationship may compromise the lender's ability to purchase a clear title at the sale. For example, the Virginia Supreme Court held that, where the trustee held 13 percent of the stock of the beneficiary and served as an officer of the beneficiary, the beneficiary's purchase was a purchase by the trustee and could thus be voided by the borrower. Whitlow v. Mountain Trust Bank, 207 S.E.2d 837 (Va. 1974). This view reflects consistency with the general rule that the trustee under a deed of trust cannot purchase at a sale it conducts, and that any such purchase can be set aside as constructively fraudulent. Smith v. Credico Industrial Loan Co., 362 S.E.2d 735 (Va. 1987); 1 Nelson & Whitman, *supra*, § 7.21, at 629.

The borrower's statutory (post-sale) right of redemption. Paragraph 43 provides that "Trustee shall deliver to the purchaser at the sale, within a reasonable time after the sale, a deed conveying the Mortgaged Property so sold with special warranty of title." (The prudent trustee would use a special warranty deed, rather than a general warranty deed, in order to avoid potential future liability for latent title defects that arose prior to the execution of the deed of trust.) In many states, where power-of-sale foreclosure statutes provide neither the borrower nor junior lienholders any post-sale redemption rights, this language poses no real concern, as the trustee could deliver a deed conveying title to the mortgaged premises without delay following completion of the sale. *See, e.g.,* Ariz. Rev. Stat. Ann. § 33-811(B) (no statutory right of redemption following a sale); Ark. Code Ann. § 18-50-108(b) (same); Idaho Code § 45-1508 (same); Rolen v. Southwest Virginia Nat'l Bank, 39 B.R. 260 (Bankr. W.D. Va. 1983) (no statutory right of redemption following a trustee's execution of a memorandum of sale under Virginia law).

In some jurisdictions, however, borrowers have either limited or extensive post-sale redemption rights that may complicate a trustee's ability to deliver clear title to the foreclosure sale purchaser. *See, e.g.,* COLO. REV. STAT. § 38-38-302 (rights for 75 days; period expanded to six months for "agricultural real estate"); MO. REV. STAT. ANN. § 443.410 (one-year redemption period, though terminated by sale unless the mortgagor gives notice of its intention to redeem at or before sale and posts bond); MICH. COMP. LAWS ANN. § 600.3240(3) (six-month redemption period for mortgage on commercial property); N.C. GEN. STAT. § 45-21.27 ("upset bid" may be filed during a ten-day period following the sale; filing of upset bid necessitates resale, prior to which borrower may redeem).

In a jurisdiction recognizing such post-sale redemption rights, a trustee's deed delivered to the purchaser prior to the end of the redemption period will be insufficient to vest complete legal title in the purchaser. In Michigan, for example, if the mortgagee purchases at the foreclosure sale, the trustee's deed does not convey any right to possession upon the mortgagee until the end of the redemption period. *See, e.g.,* Lendzion v. Senstock, 1 N.W.2d 567 (Mich. 1942).

Disbursement of proceeds: costs of sale.   Paragraph 43 provides that the trustee shall first apply the sale proceeds "to all costs and expenses of the sale, including Trustee's fees of ____% of the gross sale price, attorneys' fees and costs of title evidence." Power-of-sale foreclosure statutes take various approaches to the calculation and regulation of the trustee's fee. Some states, such as North Carolina, simply allow the trustee to collect the fee specified in the deed of trust, without any statutory maximum fee. (In North Carolina, deeds of trust typically specify a fee of 1 to 5 percent of the unpaid principal balance; nevertheless, the customary practice after default is for the lender to substitute an independent trustee and negotiate with the substitute trustee to handle the sale for an hourly fee.) Other states impose statutory maximum fee limits. *See, e.g.,* WY. ST. § 34-4-111 (fee may not exceed ten dollars—and that is not a misprint); CAL. CIV. CODE ANN. § 2924d(b) (fee may not exceed the greater of $350 or 1 percent of unpaid balance of debt). Thus, resort to the state's power-of-sale foreclosure statute may be necessary in order to evaluate the enforceability of the stipulated fee. For further guidance as to restrictions in individual states, *see* FORECLOSURE LAW & RELATED REMEDIES: A STATE-BY-STATE DIGEST (Sidney A. Keyles ed., ABA 1995).

As discussed earlier in this section, several states also impose statutory limitations upon the lender's ability to collect attorneys' fees expended in foreclosure and/or other collection efforts.

Disbursement of proceeds: satisfaction of the mortgage debt. Courts have generally held that a trustee may rely on information provided by the lender and has no duty to act independently to ascertain the truth or accuracy of that information. *See, e.g.*, Spires v. Edgar, 513 S.W.2d 372 (Mo. 1974); 1 NELSON & WHITMAN, *supra*, § 7.21, at 627. A number of state power-of-sale foreclosure statutes have expressly codified this principle. *See, e.g.*, ARIZ. REV. STAT. ANN. § 33-820(A) ("In carrying out his duties under the provisions of this chapter or any deed of trust, a trustee shall, when acting in good faith, have the absolute right to rely upon any written direction or information furnished to him by the beneficiary").

In addition to the unpaid principal balance of the mortgage debt, a lender may seek to collect additional sums pursuant to provisions authorizing the collection of default interest or involuntary prepayment charges. For example, paragraph 5 of the Deed of Trust provides that the balance of the debt shall include any prepayment fee due under the terms of the note, including "payment made after Lender's exercise of any right of acceleration of the Indebtedness." As explained in the discussion of Section 5, when the loan documents (and the note) clearly provide that a prepayment fee will apply to "involuntary" prepayments—such as the application of foreclosure sale proceeds to the accelerated debt—courts have generally enforced such provisions in accordance with the parties' agreement. *See, e.g.*, Pacific Trust Co. TTEE v. Fidelity Federal Savings & Loan Ass'n, 229 Cal. Rptr. 269 (App. 1986); Village of Rosemont v. Maywood-Proviso State Bank, 501 N.E.2d 859 (1986); Eyde v. Empire of American Federal Savings Bank, 701 F. Supp. 126 (E.D. Mich. 1988). In the event of the borrower's bankruptcy, however, the lender's ability to collect such a fee would be dependent upon the bankruptcy court's judgment that the fee was a "reasonable" charge pursuant to 11 U.S.C. § 506(b). For further discussion, *see supra* Section 5.

Likewise, paragraph 8 of the Note provides that "[s]o long as any monthly installment or any other payment due under this Note remains past due for 30 days or more, interest under this Note shall accrue on the unpaid principal balance . . . at a rate (the "Default Rate") equal to the lesser of 4 percentage points above the [stated note rate] or the maximum interest rate which may be collected from Borrower under applicable law." A significant majority of state court decisions have freely enforced contract default interest provisions (when not inconsistent with state usury limitations). *See, e.g.*, Mattvidi Associates L.P. v. NationsBank of Virginia, 639 A.2d 228 (Md. App. 1994) (collecting cases).

A recent decision of the New Jersey Superior Court, Appellate Division, Metlife Capital Financial Corp. v. Washington Ave. Assocs., L.P., 713 A.2d 527 (1998), had created significant concern among the lending community when it declared a mortgage default interest provision of 12.55 percent—3 percent over the contract interest rate of 9.55 percent—to be an unenforceable penalty rather than a valid liquidated-damages provision. In that case, the court held that the mortgagee had failed to prove that the 3 percent increase bore any relationship to the damages or actual administrative expenses incurred by the mortgagee. On June 30, 1999, however, the New Jersey Supreme Court reversed the lower court's ruling and concluded that the 3 percent rate was "a reasonable estimate of potential damages" and fell "well within the range demonstrated to be customary." Further, the court held that such a default interest provision, as a "stipulated damages clause negotiated between sophisticated commercial entities," should be treated as presumptively reasonable. Metlife Capital Financial Corp. v. Washington Ave. Assocs., L.P., 732 A.2d 493 (N.J. 1999).

Where the difference between the contract interest rate and the default rate is 4 to 6 percent or less—such as the 4 percent rate contained in paragraph 8 of the Note—it is very likely that, outside the bankruptcy context, the majority of courts will enforce the default interest rate in accordance with its terms. Where the difference between the contract interest rate and the default rate is significantly more than 4 to 6 percent, courts may view default interest provisions significantly more harshly and may be inclined to treat such provisions as an unenforceable penalty. See, e.g., Feller v. Architects Display Buildings, Inc., 148 A.2d 634 (N.J. App. 1959) (default interest rate of 33 percent—nearly twice the contract rate of 17 percent—was an unenforceable penalty).

The lender's ability to enforce a default interest provision after the borrower files for bankruptcy is less certain. During the pendency of bankruptcy, an undersecured lender is not entitled to collect interest on its secured claim at all. See 11 U.S.C. § 506(b); United Savings Ass'n of Texas v. Timbers of Inwood Forest Assocs., Ltd., 484 U.S. 365 (1988). The bankruptcy courts have split over whether an oversecured lender may collect default interest under 11 U.S.C. § 506(b) during the pendency of a bankruptcy case. Compare In re Terry Ltd. Partnership, 27 F.3d 241 (7th Cir. 1994) and In re Courtland Estates Corp., 144 B.R. 5 (Bankr. D. Mass. 1992) (default interest allowed) with In re Boulders on the River, Inc., 169 B.R. 969 (Bankr. D. Or. 1994) and In re Hollstrom, 133 B.R. 535 (Bankr. D. Colo. 1991) (default interest disallowed as unreasonable).

Disbursement of proceeds: surplus proceeds.   Any surplus proceeds of sale above the amount necessary to pay the trustee's fee and to satisfy the mortgage debt represent the remnants of the borrower's equity of redemption. As a result, this surplus constitutes proceeds of the foreclosed premises, and any now-extinguished junior liens or mortgages that had attached to the premises instead attach to the surplus. Paragraph 43 authorizes the trustee to distribute any surplus to the holders of any such extinguished junior liens according to their priority, as long as their interests are known to the trustee. The language of paragraph 43 is consistent with most power-of-sale foreclosure statutes, which either expressly authorize or have been interpreted by courts to authorize trustees to disburse surplus funds to the holders of subordinate liens rather than to the borrowers. 1 NELSON & WHITMAN, *supra*, § 7.31, at 669–670. To the extent that there is any ambiguity or uncertainty regarding the validity, enforceability, or amount of any debts owed to subordinate claimants, the prudent trustee may instead choose to pay any surplus proceeds into court, either by way of instituting an impleader action or pursuant to the express authorization (in some states) of the power-of-sale foreclosure statute. *See, e.g.,* UTAH CODE § 57-1-29 (authorizing trustee to pay surplus to the clerk of court).

Release

Upon payment of the Indebtedness, Lender shall request Trustee to release this Instrument and shall deliver the Note to Trustee. Trustee shall release this Instrument. Borrower shall pay Trustee's reasonable costs incurred in releasing this Instrument.

Explanation

Satisfaction and release of the Deed of Trust. Paragraph 44 provides a procedure for the release of the Deed of Trust and return of the Note once the entire debt is satisfied. It is important to a borrower that the title records reflect that the mortgage no longer encumbers the real estate; otherwise, it can be difficult for the borrower to obtain further financing on the property or to sell the property in the future. It would be prudent for the borrower to require the receipt of the release of the Deed of Trust from the trustee (or the release of the mortgage from the mortgagee) as a condition for making the final payment of the mortgage debt. Indeed, in the typical closing at a title company, the title company will not issue a clean title policy to the insured (a new owner or mortgage lender) unless the title company has received either such a release or (if the prior mortgagee is a known institution) a payoff statement (a statement indicating what amount is owed and necessary to pay the loan off in full).

Unfortunately, sometimes this process does not work and, after closing and the payment in full of the mortgage debt, the lender fails to provide a release to the title company or the borrower. For this reason, many states have enacted statutes to require the issuance of a release or some other procedure to clear the satisfied mortgage from the title records. See, e.g., CAL. CIV. CODE § 2941 (1998) (statute (i) requires release to be recorded within 30 days after satisfaction of debt and delivery of original note and mortgage to mortgagor upon mortgagor's written request, and (ii) contains a procedure by which a title company can record a release if the mortgagee fails to do so); 765 ILCS 905/4, 905/2 (requires mortgagee to execute release upon receiving satisfaction of lien and make release available to mortgagor within one month).

Statutes also commonly provide for damages to the party who is harmed by the mortgagee's or trustee's failure to comply with the requirements of the statute. See, e.g., CAL. CIV. CODE § 2941 (1998) (violators of statute liable for all damages to person affected by violation and shall forfeit sum of $300 to that person); UTAH CODE § 57-1-38 (3) (1985) (mortgagee or trustee who fails to release mortgage/deed of trust within 90 days after satisfaction is liable for greater of $1,000 or treble the actual damages suffered, plus attorneys' fees and court costs); 765 ILL. COMP. STAT. 905/4, 905/2 (mortgagee or trustee is liable for $200 plus reasonable attorneys' fees for violations of statute). Some courts have interpreted these statutes in a manner that is favorable to borrowers. For example, the court in Hector, Inc. v. United Savings & Loan Ass'n, 741 P.2d 542, 547 (Utah 1987), interpreted the then-existing Utah statute to provide double damages (rather than simply damages) whether the borrower had initiated a lawsuit and obtained a judgment or not (the statute was ambiguous on this point). In addition, the court in Hector calculated damages based on a 10 percent rate of interest accruing on the value of the lots that the lender should have released for the period during which the lender failed to release the lots as required by the statute. Id. at 545. Although the court in Hector recognized a "good faith" defense for lenders, the court narrowly restricted this defense to the situation of a mistaken but honest belief that the secured debt has not been satisfied in full. Id.

Because paragraph 44 merely provides a basic procedure for the release of the Deed of Trust and return of the Note, there should not be any significant enforcement issues. It should be noted, however, that the issue of releasing the Deed of Trust once the mortgage debt is paid is typically governed by state statutes that may impose some limits on the costs the trustee can recover for releasing the Deed of Trust.

In addition, there is a practical manner in which the problem of paid-off loans still appearing to encumber property can be resolved. It is common for the title insurance company that paid the mortgage lender based upon the payoff statement to provide a hold-harmless letter to the next title company that is asked to insure good title to the property. The title company will "use" the money it received to record the release to pay for the preparation of the hold-harmless letter.

Substitution of Trustee

Lender may from time to time, in Lender's discretion, remove Trustee and appoint a successor trustee to any Trustee appointed under this Instrument. Without conveyance of the Mortgaged Property, the successor trustee shall succeed to all the title, power and duties conferred upon the predecessor Trustee and by applicable law.

Explanation

Replacement or substitution of the trustee.   In the event that the original trustee dies, becomes incapacitated, or otherwise chooses not to fulfill the functions required of the trustee, paragraph 45 of the Deed of Trust allows the lender to designate a successor trustee to carry out the functions of the original trustee. Without paragraph 45, the original trustee—as the holder of an ostensible fee interest in trust for the borrower and the lender—would have to execute a conveyance of the mortgaged property to the successor trustee. This succession would be greatly complicated, of course, in the event of the trustee's death or incapacity. By virtue of paragraph 45, succession can take place without a conveyance of the mortgaged property, although prudence dictates that the lender should prepare and record a substitution-of-trustee document in order to ensure that any trustee's deed is effectively connected to the chain of title.

Conflict of interest as a necessity for substitution of the trustee. A trustee nominally holds title to the mortgaged property as a trustee for the borrower and the lender. In the event of a default by the borrower, paragraph 43 of the Deed of Trust authorizes the trustee to conduct a sale pursuant to the power of sale and to apply the proceeds of sale in the fashion specified in that paragraph. The term "trustee" carries with it conceptions of independence and strong fiduciary obligations, and there are frequently statements in the case rulings that a trustee is a fiduciary for both the lender and borrower and must act in a neutral fashion that is attentive to the interests of both parties. *See, e.g.*, Mills v. Mutual Building & Loan Ass'n, 6 S.E.2d 549 (N.C. 1940); Cox v. Helenius, 693 P.2d 683 (Wash. 1985). The notion of the trustee as fiduciary cannot be taken too far, however; because the trustee serves two parties whose interests after default are potentially in conflict, the trustee cannot be treated as a traditional fiduciary for all purposes. Instead, the nature of the trustee's "trust" is limited. The borrower can appropriately expect the trustee to carry out the obligations imposed upon it by the loan documents and the power-of-sale foreclosure statute (i.e., to give the required notices and advertisements of sale), to conduct the sale in a regular, noncollusive fashion in accordance with the notices, and to deal with the proceeds of the sale in the fashion specified by the loan documents and the governing statutes. Beyond this, courts have held that the trustee does not have a duty to investigate and confirm that the mortgage debt is actually in default, but may rely upon the lender's assertion of a default (absent actual knowledge that no default exists). *See, e.g.*, Spires v. Edgar, 513 S.W.2d 372 (Mo. 1974). Neither is the trustee obligated to investigate whether the borrower has potential claims against the lender that could be offset against the mortgage debt. *See, e.g.*, Villers v. Wilson, 304 S.E.2d 16 (1983).

As a result, because the trustee will typically be performing its duties at the behest of the lender, the lender typically designates as the original trustee a person familiar to the lender—in a number of jurisdictions, the lender may customarily designate its legal counsel—for efficiency's sake and to streamline the institution of the foreclosure process following the borrower's default.

Nevertheless, two concerns merit attention. First, courts have tended to view with some suspicion foreclosures involving an ownership or employment relationship between the trustee and the lender. For example, where a trustee owned 13 percent of the stock of the deed-of-trust beneficiary and served as one of its officers, the court concluded that the beneficiary's purchase at the sale was an indirect purchase by the trustee and could thus be voided by the borrower. Whitlow v. Mountain Trust Bank, 207 S.E.2d 837 (Va. 1974). Unless there is statutory authority authorizing the lender to serve as both beneficiary and trustee under the same deed of trust (*see, e.g.,* UTAH CODE § 57-1-21), the lender proceeding with a foreclosure would be well advised to avoid this issue altogether by substituting, if necessary, a new trustee with no significant relationship to the lender.

Second, lawyers representing lenders must recognize that serving as a trustee under the lender's deed of trust while continuing to represent the lender as its counsel creates potentially significant professional responsibility issues. In some states, statutes appear to authorize such dual service expressly. *See, e.g.,* ARIZ. REV. STAT. ANN. § 33-820(B) ("An attorney for the beneficiary shall also be qualified to act as attorney for the trustee or to be the trustee."). Other states, however, have looked at the practice with considerable suspicion. As the Washington Supreme Court suggested in *Cox v. Helenius,* 693 P.2d 683 (Wash. 1985), "[t]he spirit of [the ethical rules governing lawyers] would seem to condemn [such conduct]. Where an actual conflict of interest arises, the person serving as trustee and beneficiary should prevent a breach by transferring one role to another person." This issue has been particularly sensitive in North Carolina, where there is a significant body of state bar ethics opinions addressing this issue. In North Carolina, where power-of-sale foreclosure requires a quasi-judicial hearing before the clerk of court prior to sale, the State Bar Ethics Committee has opined that the lender's counsel may not serve as trustee under a deed of trust and also represent the lender if the borrower attempts to contest the foreclosure proceeding. RPC 82 (January 12, 1990); RPC 90 (October 17, 1990). If such a contest arises (i.e., if the borrower appears at the hearing and raises any question regarding the lender's right to foreclose), the lender's counsel must either withdraw (if he or she will continue to serve as trustee) or have the lender substitute a new trustee to avoid a conflict of interest. Furthermore, the committee has even opined that the lender's counsel cannot serve as trustee and simultaneously represent the lender in the negotiation of an "amicable modification or loan workout agreement." RPC 90 (October 17, 1990). In jurisdictions taking such a constrained view, the lender's counsel may simply choose to substitute an independent trustee under the authority of paragraph 45 of the Deed of Trust as soon as there is any indication of default under the loan documents.

Statutory Provisions

section 46

The following provisions . . . are made applicable to this Instrument: [specific state-by-state provisions omitted]

Explanation

In each state, the Fannie Mae–approved form Deed of Trust may contain certain state-specific provisions that incorporate specific state legislative provisions into the Deed of Trust. This book does not focus on any particular state and thus provides no analysis of this paragraph.

Waiver of Trial by Jury

Borrower and Lender each (a) covenants and agrees not to elect a trial by jury with respect to any issue arising out of this instrument or the relationship between the parties as Borrower and Lender that is triable of right by a jury and (b) waives any right to trial by jury with respect to such issue to the extent that any such right exists now or in the future. This waiver of right to trial by jury is separately given by each party, knowingly and voluntarily with the benefit of competent legal counsel.

Explanation

The rationale for a jury trial waiver. Paragraph 47 of the Deed of Trust provides that both the lender and the borrower agree to waive the right to a trial by jury. Lenders desire this mutual waiver of the right to a jury trial because they fear that a jury will be more disposed to find in favor of "David" than "Goliath" and to award larger verdicts to the borrower than a judge might award. This fear is based on certain infamous jury trial awards in the 1970s and 1980s. In addition, in some jurisdictions, when a party asserts the right to a jury trial, this can delay the case and lengthen the legal process. After the borrower defaults, the lender will want to exercise its remedies as quickly as possible to reduce deterioration to the mortgaged property and to mitigate its losses. Consequently, loan documents typically provide for a waiver of the right to a jury trial, similar to the one contained in paragraph 47.

Enforceability of jury trial waivers. Although the Seventh Amendment guarantees the right to a jury trial in civil cases, a contractual waiver of the right to a jury trial is effective if knowingly and voluntarily signed. *See, e.g., In re* Reggie Packing Co., 671 F. Supp. 571, 573 (N.D. Ill 1987). In order to demonstrate that the waiver was "knowing" and "voluntary," the jury waiver provision should be so obvious that a person signing the document would readily notice it, and the provision must be explained to the party making the waiver. Heller Financial, Inc. v. Finch-Bayless Equipment Co., 1990 WL 103232, *1 (N.D. Ill). Courts are divided as to which party bears the burden of proving whether an agreement to a waiver provision was knowing and voluntary. *See, e.g.,* National Equipment Rental, Ltd. v. Hendrix, 565 F. 2d 255, 258 (2d Cir. 1977) (burden rests with party seeking to enforce waiver provision); *but see* K.M.C. Co., Inc. v. Irving Trust Co., 757 F. 2d 752, 758 (6th Cir. 1985) (burden rests with party attempting to avoid enforcement of waiver provision).

Even though jury trial waivers are enforceable in theory, many courts, as one might expect, will indulge every reasonable presumption against such a waiver and place upon the lender a substantial burden in showing that the waiver was knowing, voluntary, and intentional. Aetna Ins. Co. v. Kennedy, 301 U.S. 389, 393 (1936). Connecticut courts, for example, look to the following factors in determining the validity of such waivers: (1) the conspicuousness of the waiver clause, including (a) its location relative to the signatures of the parties, (b) whether it was buried in the middle of a lengthy agreement, and (c) whether it was printed in a different typeface or font size than the remainder of the contract; (2) whether the party seeking to avoid enforcement was represented by counsel; (3) whether the same party had an opportunity to negotiate the terms of the agreement; and (4) whether the same party had been fraudulently induced into agreeing specifically to the jury trial waiver. *See, e.g.,* Happens, LLC v. Webster Bank, 1996 WL 589220, *2 (Conn. Super. 1996).

Paragraph 47 of the Deed of Trust will be enforced if it can be shown that the waiver was intentionally, knowingly, and voluntarily made. The fact that the paragraph is conspicuous (based on its location and font) and contains an acknowledgement by the parties that they consulted their own counsel with respect to the waiver increases the chances of its enforcement.

Index

223